A VISION OF SPLENDOUR

en avant · en foi · en avant · en foi ·

A VISION OF SPLENDOUR

Gothic Revival in Staffordshire
1840 - 1890

by

MICHAEL FISHER

THE AUTHOR

Michael Fisher originates from Leek, Staffordshire. After graduating in History at Leicester University he was awarded a Research Studentship at Keele where he took his Master's degree in 1967. He taught history at King Edward VI Grammar School in Stafford, and was Head of the History Department there until 1976. He has written a number of books and articles on historical and architectural themes, and edited his grandfather's military diaries for publication in 1986: *Clifford Keates, A Soldier's India.* Ordained to the priesthood in 1979, Father Michael serves at the twelfth-century church of S. Chad, Stafford. As a non-stipendiary priest, he earns his living as a self-employed artist and craftsman working with slate and natural stone, while pursuing his life-long interest in architecture and local history.

Published by the Author,
35, Newland Avenue,
Stafford. ST16 1NL

Printed by Counter Print,
3, Tipping Street,
Stafford. ST16 2LL

First Published 1995
©Michael Fisher 1995
ISBN 0 9526855 0 7

This book is respectfully dedicated
to the memory of

JOHN HILARY NEWTON

1943 - 1994

Scholar, Friend, and Founder Member of
The North Staffordshire Pevsner Society

S. Giles', Cheadle: the interior as originally envisaged by Pugin in his Dublin Review article of 1841.

Contents

AUTHOR'S PREFACE

The buildings described in this book are old friends, for I was born in Staffordshire and, apart from my undergraduate years, I have lived here almost continuously ever since. My historical research has therefore been complemented by a long-standing personal appreciation of the county's rich architectural heritage, and a commitment to its preservation. Over the years these buildings have helped to shape my architectural tastes and also my religious beliefs. They are as much a part of me as I am a part of Staffordshire.

I well remember a family outing to Alton when I was about ten years old. My mother's youngest sister, who was also my godmother, was in the party. We took the train from Leek, down the Churnet Valley Line to Oakamoor, then walked through the delightful Dimmingsdale to Alton. After a pause for refreshments we climbed to the top of Toothill, a rocky escarpment on the opposite side of the valley to the Towers. It was a warm summer's day, and both the climb and the views from the top were breathtaking. On the way down my aunt suggested a stop to look at the castle and convent, and the adjacent church of S. John. She would never go into a church with her head uncovered, so, being hatless on that occasion, she produced a lace-edged handkerchief from her handbag and put it on like a diminutive mantilla. Though not a Roman Catholic, she crossed herself with holy water from the stoup by the door, and we both lit votive candles.

That, I suppose, was my first encounter with the religion, as well as the architecture, of A.W.N. Pugin, and the memory of that day remains ever fresh: the gilded roof of the castle chapel shimmering in the bright sunlight, and the cool interior of S. John's where one of the sisters from the convent was playing soft organ music. I have returned many times since, and recently I had the privilege of talking about Pugin in the buildings which he designed, and where so many years ago I first glimpsed his vision of splendour. For me, the air of stillness and sanctity in this uniquely beautiful place is always the same, as architect and patron intended it should be.

The memory of that childhood visit may have had other consequences. Although I was born into an Anglican family, my spiritual inclinations developed in a markedly Catholic direction as I grew up. It was in the context of Gothic Revival churches that my convictions took shape, notably at All Saints', Leek, whose vicar, Fr. Norman Turner, first acquainted me with the incense-laden atmosphere of Bodley's fine church at Hoar Cross.

I suspect there may be an hereditary element too. My aunt's familiarity with Catholic practices owed much to the Revd. Jasper Stoneman Caiger, who was vicar of S. Edward's, Leek, just after the First World War, and later of Denstone, another destination of family outings. My grandmother was particularly fond of him because of his kindness to her family at the time of my grandfather's death. He was a committed Anglo-Catholic, and his time in Leek was cut short by those who disliked his brand of churchmanship, but he was there long enough to influence the religious upbringing of my mother and her sisters.

As a budding historian in the 1960s I began to take an interest in visiting and recording Staffordshire churches, and in my student days at Leicester University I had the opportunity to extend my architectural interests by doing the rounds of the charming villages of Leicestershire and Rutland. I chose mid-Victorian England as a topic, and this inevitably included the Gothic Revival. One of my tutors at Leicester was totally sceptical, in those days before Pevsner's *Staffordshire* was in print, about the architectural merits of my home county, so I showed him pictures of All Saints', Leek, and took him on a visit to Hoar Cross. He quickly changed his mind.

S. Mary's, Stafford, is the principal church of the parish in which I have lived for the past twenty-seven years, and where I have served as a priest since 1979. In 1985 I was asked by the rector to write a new guide book for S. Mary's. The research for this unearthed far more material than it was possible to use, and it radically altered my opinion of George Gilbert Scott as a church restorer. Scott's own account of his work at S. Mary's reveals him to have been far more sensitive, both to the views of his opponents, and to the merits of architectural styles other than his beloved Gothic, than later critics and detractors have given him credit for. S. Mary's is therefore a key building in which to assess the significance of a great architect and conservationist who has been unjustly maligned. But for Gilbert Scott neither S. Mary's nor a good many other of our great churches and cathedrals would still be standing today.

Starting with my own re-appraisal of Sir Gilbert Scott, I began to realise that Staffordshire had played a particularly important part in the Gothic Revival through the architects and patrons of buildings I had known in some instances from my childhood days. Out came the notebooks, sketches and photographs of earlier years, and here is the result, supplemented of course by more recent research.

Now seems an opportune time for such a book. Thanks to recent and careful restoration work, some of these buildings look better than they have done for many years. Pugin's banqueting hall at Alton Towers is once more accessible to the public, as is the chapel, with its fine ceiling freshly painted and re-gilded. The stunning interior of S. Giles', Cheadle, has benefited from cleaning and the installation of a new lighting system, and 1996 will see the 150th anniversary of the consecration of "Pugin's Gem". Work carried out at All Saints', Leek, in the Spring of 1994 restored pristine freshness to Gerald Horsley's paintings and decorations in the chancel, those on the ceiling being properly illuminated for the first time. Equally important is the fact that all five of the splendid churches surveyed in this book are very much alive and in use as places of worship, proclaiming the faith which inspired their founders and architects to create them. The future too seems promising. Alton Castle, which has lain empty for several years, has undergone a certain amount of repair and conservation work, and it is hoped that a new and appropriate role will soon be found for this, one of Pugin's most important buildings. It would seem that Gothic Revival art and architecture are being viewed much more positively than was the case even a few decades ago, and it is to be hoped that Staffordshire will receive due recognition as both cradle and finishing-school of this great movement as modern-day visitors share the vision of splendour which Pugin and several of his followers expressed here so magnificently.

MICHAEL FISHER
14th September 1995
Holy Cross Day, and the 143rd anniversary of the death of A.W.N. Pugin

ACKNOWLEDGEMENTS

I am grateful to all who have helped in any way by answering my queries, locating source-materials and pictures, and allowing me to take photographs. Particular thanks are due to Fr. Bede Walsh, parish priest of S. Giles', Cheadle, to the Revd. Gordon Mursell (S. Mary's, Stafford) for permission to reproduce S. Mary's archive material held on deposit at the Staffordshire County Record Office; to the Revd. Jonathan Clatworthy (All Saints', Denstone), Canon Henry Hughes (Hoar Cross), and the Revd. Jonathan Eades (All Saints', Leek); also to Sir Patrick Cormack, F.S.A., M.P. I am deeply grateful to the Professional Authors' and Publishers' Association for their invaluable help and advice over the publication and promotion of this book. Finally I wish to thank my wife Isobel who has accompanied me on many visits to the various buildings and given helpful advice in the choice and preparation of illustrative material.

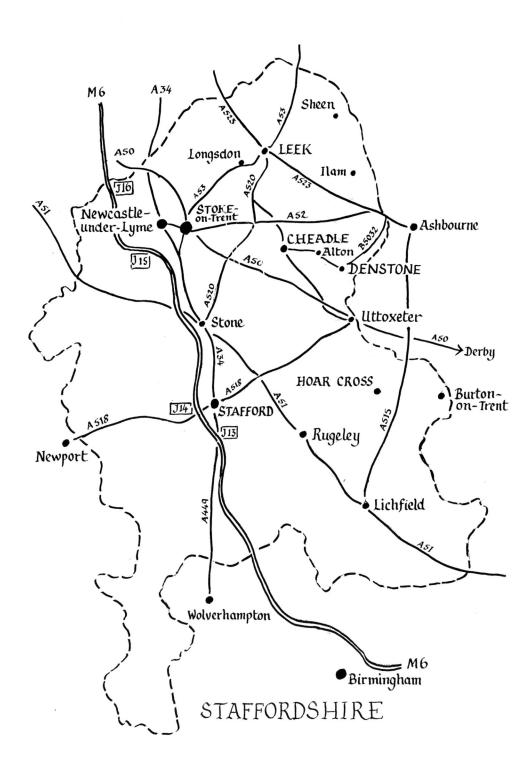

STAFFORDSHIRE

1   Frontispiece designed by A.W.N. Pugin for John Masfen's **Views of the Church of St.
Mary at Stafford** *(1852) showing the window, also designed by Pugin, given to
S. Mary's in memory of John Masfen who died in 1846.*

2 & 3: S. Giles', Cheadle: the Blessed Sacrament Chapel, and the Easter Sepulchre

16

4   All Saints', Denstone - the pulpit

5 All Saints', Leek - altar-frontal designed by Norman Shaw and executed by the Leek School of Needlework, c 1887

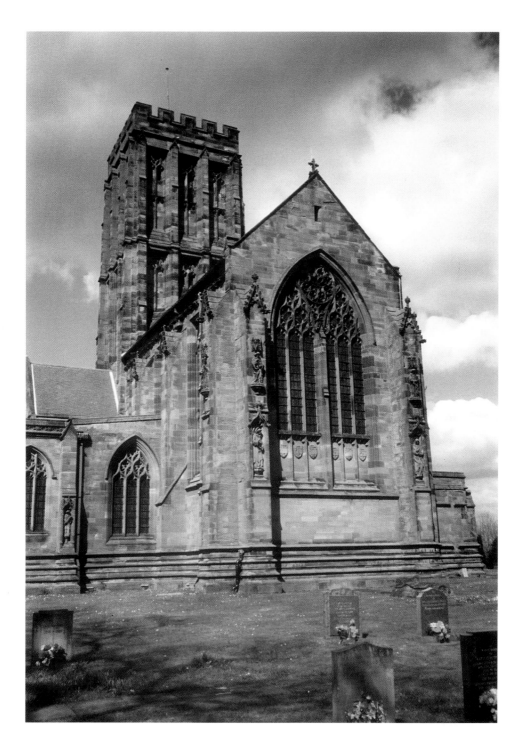

6 Church of the Holy Angels, Hoar Cross, from the east.

INTRODUCTION

Staffordshire was the last volume to appear in the late Sir Nikolaus Pevsner's *Buildings of England* series (Penguin Books 1974). Before its publication people who had little knowledge of the county joked that Pevsner had left it until last because he couldn't think what to put in it, and that *Staffordshire* was bound to be the slimmest volume of the entire series. After all, it was said that Queen Victoria ordered the blinds of the royal train to be closed when passing through parts of the county, so dismal was the outlook, and there still may be those who think of Staffordshire as the Potteries in the north, the Black Country in the south, and nothing worth looking at in between.

Pevsner's *Staffordshire* is not the slim volume that sceptics predicted, and Sir Nikolaus had his own personal reasons for wishing it to be the one with which to conclude the series. More importantly, it helped to show that Staffordshire's heritage of fine buildings is as rich and varied as that of any other Midland county, and even the industrial areas hold their surprises.

The county's legacy of Victorian Gothic Revival buildings is particularly rich. In north-east Staffordshire alone four architects of national repute designed what are acknowledged to be the finest buildings of their kind: A.W.N. Pugin at Cheadle and Alton, G.E. Street at Denstone, and R.N. Shaw at Leek; while a little to the south is G.F. Bodley's masterpiece, the Church of the Holy Angels at Hoar Cross. Nor is this all. Had the blinds of the royal train been raised when passing through Stafford Station, Queen Victoria might have caught a glimpse of the pinnacled tower of S. Mary's, endowed as a Collegiate Church by her ancestor King John, and restored in the early 1840s by a young architect whose name is forever linked with the Gothic Revival - George Gilbert Scott. Not only was S. Mary's his first significant piece of restoration work and the one which established Scott's reputation as a church architect, it was the first restoration of a major church along the lines advocated by the newly-formed Camden Society which Scott joined in the year he began work in Stafford. Far from being a back-water, Staffordshire was in the very forefront of the religious and architectural movements which by the end of the century had transformed the Victorian Church beyond recognition.

In 1836 A.W.N. Pugin's satirical book, *Contrasts*, sounded the clarion-call of the Gothic Revival, and there was more to come. A recent convert to both Roman Catholicism and Gothic architecture, Pugin denounced as pagan and foreign the neo-Classicism and the Italianate furnishings of English Catholic churches. Though they may not have agreed with his conclusion that Gothic led inevitably to the Church of Rome, many Anglicans responded eagerly to Pugin's call to study Gothic architecture, for they considered it to be a rightful part of the heritage of the Church of England. Architects needed to learn how to build properly in this style, which had been neglected since the Reformation, for most of what passed as "Gothic" in the early nineteenth century was in fact a sham; a thin veneer of ornament applied to buildings which in matters of structure were not Gothic at all.

Among those who responded to the call to make a serious study of Gothic architecture were J.M. Neale, A.J. Beresford Hope, and Benjamin Webb. In 1839 they formed the Cambridge Camden Society (or Ecclesiological Society) "to promote the study of Ecclesiological architecture and the restoration of mutilated architectural remains". Just as Pugin despised the "foreign" and "pagan" architectural fashions of the Church of Rome, so the

Ecclesiologists poured scorn on the eighteenth- and early nineteenth-century setting of Anglican worship - the box-pews, galleries, prominent pulpits and neglected altars which made the interiors of many parish churches barely distinguishable from those of Nonconformist chapels. While the Oxford Movement under Newman, Keble and Pusey attempted to renew the Catholicity of the Church of England on an inward and spiritual plane, the Cambridge Ecclesiologists aimed at restoring the beauty of holiness through the renovation and re-furnishing of old churches, and the building of new ones in a Gothic style based on proper understanding of architectural principles, and thorough research. The tone of the Society became increasingly Anglo-Catholic, advocating the re-introduction into the Church of England of long-forgotten ornaments, furnishings and ritual practices, many of which were frowned upon as smacking of "popery".

That Staffordshire should have been in the forefront of these movements might seem strange at first sight, but it becomes less strange once it is known that Ecclesiology found early sympathisers and active supporters among a number of wealthy Staffordshire families who were prepared to open their purses. A.J. Beresford Hope, "the Nestor of Ecclesiology", was a Staffordshire landowner whose properties included the patronage of the church at Sheen, a tiny village in the northern Moorlands. In 1853 he gave the living to fellow-ecclesiologist and Secretary of the Camden Society, Benjamin Webb, and Webb engaged William Butterfield to complete the rebuilding of the church. They even planned to turn Sheen into an "Anglo-Catholic watering-place", complete with Choir School and Reformatory, but progressed no further than building the church and vicarage. The significance of the Sheen experiment should not, however, be underestimated, for within a few years the Butterfield-Beresford Hope partnership produced the model church of the Ecclesiological Movement - All Saints' Margaret Street, London -

8 & 9: Ilam, a North Staffordshire village rich in Gothic Revival architecture. The Watts Russell memorial chapel (1831) on the north side of the church, and the memorial cross erected by Jesse Watts Russell in 1840.

complete with its Choir School and vicarage. A new home was found at S. Luke's Sheen for some of the furnishings from the old Margaret Chapel, and in the 1970s Sheen vicarage won new fame as the very last building to be surveyed by Pevsner for the very last volume of *The Buildings of England.*

A near neighbour of the Beresford Hopes was Jesse Watts Russell of Ilam Hall, who was experimenting with Gothic a decade or more before Pugin and the Ecclesiologists. In the early 1820s he rebuilt the hall in a fanciful style, and in 1831 he added a rib-vaulted octagonal chapel to the north side of Ilam church - neo-Perpendicular in style, and for its date a remarkably serious piece of Gothic Revival. The Ecclesiologists would have condemned both: the hall as sham Gothic and the chapel as debased Gothic, for they scorned Perpendicular. Yet in 1840 Watts Russell built, in the centre of Ilam village, a memorial cross inspired by the same monuments from which Gilbert Scott developed his Oxford Martyrs' Memorial a year later - the "Eleanor Crosses" of Edward I which the Ecclesiologists would certainly have admired. It is difficult to escape the conclusion that Jesse Watts Russell had, by 1840, fallen under the spell of the Camden Society. What we do know for certain is that in 1841 he made an extremely generous offer of £5,000 to restore the interior of a Staffordshire church along Camdenian lines, and there was a willing recipient - the Revd William Coldwell of S. Mary's at Stafford. S. Mary's had already been surveyed by George Gilbert Scott, but Coldwell lacked the money necessary to save it from almost certain collapse. Watts Russell's gift coincided with Scott's conversion to Ecclesiology, and the Camden Society became actively involved with his pioneering restoration work at Stafford's Collegiate Church.

Meanwhile, Scott's new mentor, A.W.N. Pugin, was making his mark in north-east Staffordshire, an area so rich in Pugin buildings that there is no better place in which to study him. Only in Staffordshire did Pugin come close to realising the visions of Catholic England set out in *Contrasts* and elsewhere, for his patron was England's premier Catholic earl, and Staffordshire landowner, Lord Shrewsbury, who shared Pugin's visions and had ample funds with which to finance them. As a consequence Pugin's chapels at Alton Castle and Cotton College are on a grand scale, while S. Giles' Roman Catholic Church at Cheadle realises his vision of splendour like no other church he ever built. "Perfect Cheadle", he was to call it, "my consolation in all my afflictions."

Among the Anglican families who built churches where none had existed before were the Heywoods, whose fortunes were made in Manchester banks, and who were enthusiastic supporters of the Anglo-Catholic revival. In 1860 Thomas Percival Heywood commissioned the young George Edmund Street to design a church, vicarage and school for his home village of Denstone. The result was exactly the kind of "Athens in the Moorlands" that Butterfield and Webb had envisaged at Sheen, and the influence of All Saints', Margaret Street was much in evidence, for Street worshipped there, and was soon to be one of its wardens. Denstone is one of Street's very best churches, in the Middle Pointed style favoured by Scott and the ecclesiologists, but also original in design and use of materials. It is full of surprises.

Surprising also is the church of the Holy Angels at Hoar Cross, built by George Frederick Bodley in 1872-76. That so tiny a community should have such a large and splendid church was due entirely to the unbounded generosity of Mrs Emily Charlotte Meynell-Ingram, whose brother, Charles Lindley Wood (later 2nd Viscount Halifax), was President of the leading Anglo-Catholic society, the English Church Union. No expense was spared, and so Hoar Cross, with its wealth of ornament and detail, represents the very perfection of Christian architecture as Pugin had envisaged it. Yet Hoar Cross is an Anglican church. As a zealous young convert to Roman Catholicism Pugin had doubted if Gothic could ever be revived successfully within the Church of England. In later life he began to concede that it might, and Hoar Cross, had he lived to see it, would have convinced him utterly.

Silk-manufacturers rather than aristocracy and landed gentry provided funds for the building of All Saints' Leek (1885-87). Whether or not shrewd business sense influenced the Building Committee, it succeeded in obtaining a more capacious church than Hoar Cross, at a fraction of the cost. It is the finest of the sixteen churches designed by Richard Norman Shaw, and its interior furnishings and décor are of considerable significance in the early history of the Arts and Crafts Movement.

The success of Norman Shaw's work at Leek owed much to the harmonious partnership between a renowned architect and a local builder. The builder's detailed diaries offer a rare day-to-day insight into the construction of a great Victorian church and into his own working relationship with Norman Shaw. Equally well-documented is Scott's restoration of S. Mary's, Stafford, through a series of drawings made by local artists before and after, Scott's own account of what he did there, and the correspondence which passed between rector, architect and the Ecclesiological Societies as the work progressed. Denstone church possesses a large scrap-book filled with a wealth and variety of sources covering the first thirty years of its life, which were of far more than local significance. All of this gives added interest to this fine heritage of buildings which, it is hoped, readers will wish to explore and enjoy at first-hand.

No account of the Gothic Revival in Staffordshire would be complete without reference to the two industries which in the eighteenth and nineteenth centuries made the north of the county nationally and internationally famous: ceramics and textiles. Both of these industries made significant contributions to the interiors of Gothic Revival buildings - and those of other styles and periods too - in Staffordshire and much further afield.

In the 1840s a partnership grew between Pugin and the Stoke-on-Trent pottery manufacturer Herbert Minton. Just as Pugin relied on the technical ability of John Hardman of Birmingham to execute his designs in metalwork and glass, so he found in Herbert Minton a man with sufficient personal interest and technical skill to revive the medieval processes of encaustic tile manufacture, which involved pouring liquid clay, or ''slip'', of a contrasting colour into indented patterns on a prepared base tile. Nineteenth-century technology enabled Minton and Pugin to go beyond a mere revival of medieval patterns and methods to develop finely-finished multi-coloured tiles with more intricate designs and with a higher degree of accuracy than anything that the Middle Ages could have produced. Though his patterns were inspired by medieval examples, when it came to the actual execution of them Pugin had no qualms about using the most up-to-date and sophisticated methods available to the mid-nineteenth-century ceramics industry. Thus it was possible to create the glowing compositions of encaustic floor tiles and block-printed wall tiles seen, for example, at S. Giles', Cheadle, where tiles of different shapes, sizes and patterns fit together with jigsaw-like accuracy. Like his partnership with Hardman, Pugin's association with Herbert Minton developed into a personal friendship broken only by Pugin's death in 1852, by which time Minton's ceramics had been displayed to great effect at the Great Exhibition, and since Pugin was responsible for the interior design of the Palace of Westminster, specially-commissioned Minton tiles are seen there in great profusion.

Many Anglican churches in north Staffordshire claim to have "Pugin" tiles, including All Saints', Leigh, not far from Cheadle, a remarkable piece of Camdenian Gothic by a little-known architect, Thomas Johnson of Lichfield (1845). The chancel tiles here are particularly rich, and the Pugin influence is unmistakable. Minton did, of course, supply tiles to other architects. Surviving pattern books in the Minton Museum in Stoke-on-Trent show what was available, and Pugin's name is firmly attached to a number of these. Among the Anglican churches of the period, two in particular stand out for their use of Minton ceramics: Holy Trinity, Hartshill, which Gilbert Scott built at the expense of the Minton family, and S. Mary's, Stafford. The tiles used by Scott at S. Mary's were provided largely at Herbert Minton's own expense. One could be cynical and say that since this was the first significant restoration of a medieval church along Camdenian lines, Minton had a vested interest in securing orders for the many more that would follow! At S. Mary's the whole of the vast chancel floor is covered in encaustic tiles, rising by stages - each one defined by a different pattern of tiles - towards the altar which is backed by a dado of multi-coloured tiles in rich geometrical patterns and a frieze depicting the instruments of the Passion picked out in gold and blue.

Between the twelfth and the fifteenth centuries the manufacture of ecclesiastical textiles gave England an international reputation, the name *opus anglicanum* ("English work") being universally applied to the superb embroideries done in silk and silver-gilt thread for such items as Mass vestments, copes, palls and altar-frontals, mainly in London workshops. Then came the Reformation, which witnessed the confiscation and destruction of vestments as part of the wholesale pillage which robbed English churches and cathedrals of most of their fine heritage of ecclesiastical art in all its many forms. Such examples of *opus anglicanum* as survived were preserved in English Catholic families for occasional clandestine use, or in Catholic Europe where some items were held in sufficiently high esteem to ensure their preservation until the present day. It was to these surviving examples, and to illustrations in medieval illuminated manuscripts and on old memorial brasses, that the leaders of the Gothic Revival turned when seeking to revive a long-lost art. Pugin wanted to re-introduce vestments of the true Gothic shape and style, as distinct from the Latin and Baroque forms currently in use in the Catholic church. Anglican Catholics sought to introduce similar items into a Church where eucharistic vestments had not been in general use for three hundred years.

Most of Pugin's ecclesiastical textiles were produced from woven silks, brocaded fabrics and woven braids produced in factories in Manchester and Halifax, and made up largely in the Hardman workshops in Birmingham. Many fine examples are now housed in the Victoria and Albert Museum, and at S. Mary's College, Oscott, though some are still in use, for instance at S. Giles' Cheadle.

Staffordshire was particularly fortunate in that, by the time various battles had been fought over the legality of vestments in the Church of England, local silk-manufacturers and local embroiderers had developed techniques and skills that were set to take this particular art-form beyond anything that Pugin had been able to achieve, and even to match the original *opus anglicanum* of the Middle Ages. In the 1880s and '90s the products of the Leek silk mills, and "Leek Embroidery" worked with locally-dyed *tussore* silk from India and metallic gold thread, made a great impact in exhibitions all over the country, and overseas. Whereas Pugin had relied heavily on machine-woven braids to decorate his vestments, Leek embroidery was carried out exclusively by hand, to designs inspired by medieval examples, or supplied by notable architects. The altar frontals still in use or on display in the Leek churches are probably the most magnificent of the items made by the Leek School of Art Embroidery which was encouraged and financed by the silk-manufacturers themselves. Along with the ceramic products of the Minton factory, these locally-produced textiles highlight the unique role of north Staffordshire in the history of the Gothic Revival.

10 & 11   North Staffordshire skills which made a distinctive contribution both locally and nationally to the Gothic Revival: Ceramic tiles by Herbert Minton at S. Giles', Cheadle, and hand-embroidered silk vestments at All Saints', Leek.

12 *George Gilbert Scott, drawn by George Richmond
(Frontispiece to Scott's* **Personal and Professional
Recollections** *published in 1879)*

SIR GEORGE GILBERT SCOTT AND THE RESTORATION OF S. MARY'S, STAFFORD

"The Church's restoration,
In eighteen eighty-three,
Has left for contemplation
Not what there used to be."

John Betjeman

There is no doubt that when George Gilbert Scott died in 1878 the Church of England was both inwardly and outwardly different from what it had been in the days of his youth. When Scott was a young man of twenty-one, Dr. Thomas Arnold, the celebrated Headmaster of Rugby School, pronounced: "The Church as it now stands, no human power can save". Methodism had tried to revive it, but had been effectively forced to seek a separate identity because Anglican bishops frowned upon its spiritual zeal as "a very horrid thing". Meanwhile, Evangelicals who remained within the Church of England transformed individual souls and individual parishes, but had little to say about the renewal of the Church as a divine institution. Many bishops did not reside in their dioceses, and more than half of England's 11,000 parishes had non-resident priests.

The atmosphere of neglect and decay was mirrored in the poor state of many church buildings and in the misconduct of public worship. In the mid-1870s Scott's contemporary, W.E. Gladstone, looked back to scenes which both remembered with equal revulsion:

"The actual state of things was bad beyond all parallel known to me in experience or reading. Taking together the expulsion of the poor and labouring classes (especially from the town churches), the mutilations and blockages of the fabrics, the baldness of the service, the elaborate horrors of the so-called music, with the jargon of the parts contrived to exhibit the powers of every village roarer, and to prevent all congregational singing; and, above all, the coldness and indifference of the lounging or sleeping congregations, our services were probably without parallel in the world for their debasement." (1)

Equally serious was the failure to provide more churches for the growing population of the towns. In North Staffordshire only seven new churches were built between 1600 and 1800, while existing churches were crowded with galleries and extra pews, often resulting in the kind of mutilations and blockages to which Gladstone referred. In some extreme cases, for example S. Peter's Stoke in 1826 and S. Giles' Cheadle in 1837, the problems posed by lack of accommodation and the ruinous state of the existing fabric were solved by wholesale demolition and rebuilding. In Staffordshire as elsewhere in the country, the new churches of the early nineteenth century were fairly uniform in plan and furnishing: the so-called "Commissioners' Churches" with enclosed west towers, galleries, minimal chancels, and the altar obscured by a "three-decker" pulpit standing on the centre line of the church. As for architectural style, the same basic structure could be made to appear "Classical" or "Gothic" simply by changing the shape of the windows, pillars, arches and doorways. (2)

By the 1870s Anglican worship and its architectural setting had experienced profound changes resulting from the twofold impact of the Tractarian Movement and the Gothic Revival, and no name has been more closely linked with the latter than that of Sir George

Gilbert Scott. Out of the twenty-six cathedrals of the old and monastic foundations only three were untouched by Scott, and at least 800 parish churches were either restored or built anew from his office. At his funeral in Westminster Abbey Dean Stanley remarked, "...no name within the last thirty years has been so widely impressed on the edifices of Great Britain, past and present, as that of Sir Gilbert Scott".

It was not, however, as a builder of churches that Scott began his architectural career, but as a designer of a very different kind of Victorian institution - the workhouse. The Poor-Law Guardians' concern with economy allowed him little scope for architectural refinement in these Dickensian establishments, and in later years Scott was much ashamed of them. Yet it was a Poor-Law Commissioner who first acquainted Scott with the rector of S. Mary's, Stafford: one of a series of coincidences which led not only to the restoration of S. Mary's, but through it to a new career as the most prolific church builder and restorer of the century.

Between 1836 and 1845 the London-based partnership of G.G. Scott and W.B. Moffatt designed fifty-three workhouses for the newly-established Poor-Law Unions in various parts of the country. This involved much travelling, and it was on one of these journeys in 1838 that Scott met the Assistant Poor-Law Commissioner for Staffordshire and Derbyshire, Thomas Stevens, whom he described as a freak of nature amongst Poor-Law Commissioners on account of his being a lover of Gothic architecture, a sound churchman, a prospective ordinand, and a daily worshipper at Lichfield Cathedral. (3) Their chance meeting at Uttoxeter resulted in a lasting friendship, and in 1840 Stevens wrote to inform Scott that the Revd W.E. Coldwell, rector of S. Mary's Stafford, was anxious to restore his dilapidated church if only he could raise sufficient funds. On Stevens' suggestion, Scott wrote to Coldwell offering to inspect the church and make out a report on what needed to be done. The offer was immediately taken up, but Coldwell's appeal for the necessary money brought such a pathetic response from the people of Stafford that he despaired of saving S. Mary's from almost certain collapse.

Within days of leaving the disheartened Mr. Coldwell, Stevens received a letter from Jesse Watts Russell of Ilam Hall asking his advice as to how a sum of £5,000 might best be used for church-building or restoration, and expressing a preference for Staffordshire. Stevens had no hesitation in recommending S. Mary's, Stafford, with the result that Watts Russell authorised him to tell Coldwell that £5,000 was available for the restoration of the interior of the church, on condition that public subscriptions amounting to £3,000 should be raised for work on the exterior. Coldwell's second appeal was more successful than the first, so that within a few weeks of being without funds and without hope, he was able to prepare for the actual commencement of the work, with Scott as the architect.

Scott admitted that these were early days of church restoration, and that he claimed no credit for acting upon any accurately-defined principle. (4) As a boy he had visited and sketched old churches in his native Buckinghamshire, and as a result had developed a love of Gothic architecture, but up to 1841 his practical experience as a church builder and restorer was very limited. He built his first church (at Lincoln) in 1838, and about half a dozen others followed over the next two years. None of them had chancels, most had galleries, and the mouldings and even some of the pillars were of plaster. Scott looked back on these buildings with horror:

"... As I had not yet awaked to the viciousness of shams, I was unconscious of the abyss into which I had fallen. These days of abject degradation lasted for about two years or little more, but, alas! what a mass of horrors was perpetrated during this short interval!

Often, and that within a few months of this period, have I been wicked enough to wish my works burnt down again." (5)

For one so inexperienced in matters of ecclesiastical taste or ritual propriety, the restoration of a major church like S. Mary's Stafford was a formidable challenge; yet by 1842 - the year in which the work began - Scott had undergone what can only be described as a conversion. In the first place, having caught sight of an article by Benjamin Webb, Secretary of the recently-formed Camden Society, he arranged a meeting with Webb, became a regular reader of the Society's journal, *The Ecclesiologist*, and in 1842 joined the Society itself. Secondly, Scott read A.W.N. Pugin's articles in the *Dublin Review* on the current state of church architecture. They excited him almost to fury, and, having once met this morning star of the Gothic Revival, Scott acquired an insatiable appetite for everything that Pugin said, or wrote, or built.

"I suddenly found myself like a person awakened from a long feverish dream, which had rendered him unconscious of what was going on about him..... I was in fact a new man." (6)

While still in the awakening stage, Scott competed successfully for the design of the Martyrs' Memorial at Oxford, and he re-fitted the interior of Chesterfield church - a project which gave him little satisfaction, partly because he was obliged to provide galleries, something which all true Ecclesiologists abhorred. By the time his plans for S. Mary's were ready, Scott was fully awake, and he approached the task with all the zeal of a new convert.

Even for county town like Stafford, S. Mary's is a very large church: 178 feet in length, cruciform in plan, with nave and chancel of almost equal size separated by a central tower. Dating, in its oldest parts, from about 1200, S. Mary's had been a Collegiate Church, and this explains its size and plan. Until 1548 the transepts and unusually large chancel were the preserve of a college of prebends, whose duties included praying for living and departed members of the Royal Family. Some of them lived in small houses around the church, and even today the precincts of S. Mary's retain the atmosphere of a small cathedral close. The nave served as Stafford's parish church, with its separate altar, and it was divided from the chancel and transepts by screens, portions of which were still *in situ* in 1840. The College was dissolved under the Suppression of Chantries Act of 1548, but S. Mary's continued as a parish church, with one of the former prebends as its vicar. In 1571 the status of S. Mary's was formally settled by Queen Elizabeth I who gave revenues from the former Collegiate property to the Borough Corporation on condition that they should pay the rector, as he was now to be called, and maintain the fabric of the church in good order.

The history of the fabric of S. Mary's from the late sixteenth century onwards is nevertheless one of neglect, slow decay, and accidental damage. Until 1593 the octagonal tower carried a graceful spire - said to have been one of the tallest in the country - but in the high winds of that year the spire collapsed "at twice", causing considerable damage to the chancel and south transept. The chancel had never, of course, been a part of the "parochial" church, and when the Rector asked for repairs to be done to it in 1639 the Borough Corporation proposed to demolish it completely, and wall up the tower arches. The rector objected to this, and after an appeal the Lord Keeper ruled that, under the Queen Elizabeth grant of 1571, the Corporation was obliged to repair both nave and chancel (7). Nevertheless, by 1777 the church was in such bad repair that it had to be closed for a time, and by 1837 so much needed to be done that Archdeacon Hodson instructed the churchwardens to have the fabric examined by a good architect and to submit his report. Nothing was done for another three years, at which point Scott came on the scene, under the circumstances previously described.

Recalling his first visit to S. Mary's, Scott wrote,

"The exterior was dilapidated and decayed: in one part overhanging and threatening to fall, or supported in a temporary manner by friendly but uncouth buttresses; in another, disfigured by reckless injuries or incongruous additions; some windows blocked up, others filled with rude tracery not their own; and nearly every part showing the unsparing hand of time, or the more ruthless ravages of mutilation." (8)

The most serious practical problem was the central tower. The four massive piers which supported it had been built, in about 1200, with a core of rubble set in mortar and cased in stone. Over the centuries the mortar had perished, so the whole weight of the tower was being carried by the casing. Some of the piers had been shored with rough stonework to give additional strength, and on the north side one of the nave arches had been walled up for the same purpose. Burials which had taken place near the pillars had disturbed the subsoil on which they rested, and the whole structure was perilously unstable.

The interior of S. Mary's was, according to Scott, a hideous chamber of horrors far worse than he had seen elsewhere. The aisles were filled up with galleries, the fronts of which projected outwards beyond the nave pillars so that the capitals were completely enclosed. On investigation, Scott found that the capitals had been largely cut away and that the pillars and arches had been mutilated to make way for the gallery staircases. Niches had been cut into some of the pillars to provide resting-places for the heads of those who sat there. The west end of the nave was crossed by a gallery of enormous depth, and at the back of this was the organ, which rose almost to ceiling level. The nave itself was filled with box-pews of various shapes and sizes, and since the pulpit stood immediately in front of the west gallery, most of these seats faced west rather than east. Though the nave was completely cluttered, the transepts were virtually empty and the chancel was used only for the monthly celebration of the Holy Communion.

Scott's gloomy description of S. Mary's is confirmed by a contemporary drawing and by a guide-book that was produced at about the same time for travellers on the new railway:-

"...There is every sign of decay and not one of care or attention. It would be beautiful as a ruin, but as a place of worship it is disgraceful... There is a service twice on Sundays, but one would suppose that neither the clerk, organist nor singers ever received anything for their services, they perform them so miserably."

A colony of bats hung from the roof of the nave, and if disturbed they swept down on the oil lamps that lit the church during services.

It has to be said, of course, that the internal arrangement of S. Mary's, with its galleries, box-pews, and the pulpit as the focal-point of the church, perfectly expressed the state of Anglican worship in the early nineteenth century when the emphasis was on the spoken word, not the performance of a grand liturgy, and when many churches had only a quarterly celebration of the Holy Communion. In most ancient churches, therefore, the chancel was a largely redundant feature, but by the 1840s this was beginning to change. As the Oxford Tractarians dwelt upon the doctrinal continuity of the Church of England with its medieval predecessor, so the Cambridge Ecclesiologists nursed the ritual solemnities which survived the Reformation and which, though largely ignored, were embodied in the 1662 Prayer Book. Rubrics directing that "chancels shall remain as they have done in times past", and that such ornaments and vestments as were customary in 1548-9 "shall be retained and be in use" were but two of the long-neglected requirements of the Prayer Book. In matters of ornaments and furnishings, the Ecclesiologists settled on 1550 as their ideal: a year in which, although doctrinally reformed, the Church of England was still manifestly Catholic in its practices. In matters of construction, however, they agreed with Pugin that the early fourteenth century marked the high point of Christian architecture. Unlike Pugin, they believed that the Church of England was the rightful heir of this architectural heritage which needed to be re-discovered, studied, restored and revived.

By 1842 Gilbert Scott was on the point of joining the Camden Society, and so his re-ordering of the interior of S. Mary's accorded with their developing ideas and was arguably the first of its kind. Out went the assortment of box-pews, to be replaced by open benches in the nave and aisles, all facing east. (9) Down came the galleries, organ and pulpit. The organ was removed to the north aisle of the chancel, and a new pulpit was sited by the north-west pier of the tower. The chancel itself was opened up so that the choir could be restored to what the Ecclesiologists argued was its original and proper place. The altar, rather than the pulpit, was now the focal point of the building, raised on steps against an east wall clad in Minton tiles, under a stained-glass window given by Jesse Watts Russell, and covered with a cloth of crimson velvet richly embroidered by his daughters. When the church was re-opened in December 1844 the congregation returned to surroundings vastly different from the ones they had left two years previously, and to a style of worship "more in accordance with that usually observed in Collegiate churches." (10) The choir appeared in surplices, only three years after the Revd W.F. Hook had caused a major upheaval by introducing a surpliced choir at Leeds Parish Church.

13   Oil painting of the Revd. W.E. Coldwell, Rector of S. Mary's, Stafford, 1820-1867 (Staffs. County Record Office)

14 S. Mary's, Stafford, in about 1800, drawn from an original water-colour in the William Salt Library, Stafford. The building in the foreground is the old church of S. Bertelin, demolished in 1801.

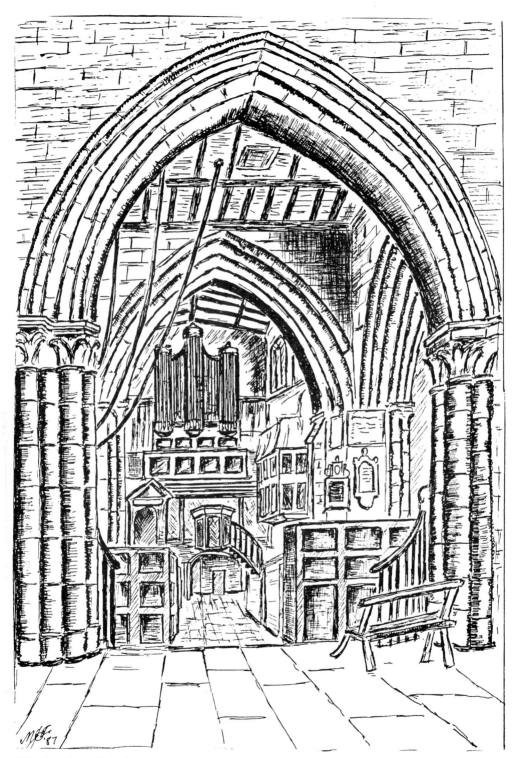

15　Interior of S. Mary's looking west, c. 1827.　Drawing from photograph of original painting (now lost) by Robert Flamank.　Staffs. County Record Office.

43

The internal arrangements were the easiest part of Scott's task. More challenging, and indeed dangerous, was the restoration of the fabric, and in particular the tower. After removing all the graves and loose earth in the vicinity of the crossing piers, Scott laid down a solid concrete "raft" all around the piers and under the tower, and then constructed a system of bearing shores resting on the concrete to support the tower arches while the piers were repaired. Little by little the old decayed stonework and perished core of each pier was renewed. In some places it was necessary to remove the old work to a depth of four feet from the surface, so that by the time the masons had worked completely around each pier, very little was left of the old core. Scott directed that the hardest stone obtainable should be used. The superstructure of the tower and octagon was stabilised with iron cramps, and metal bondings were inserted into the new stonework of the piers. This additional strength was vital because Scott's plan included the rebuilding of the spire, which was to be of stone.

The south wall of the chancel was leaning so badly that Scott decided to demolish and rebuild. Much of the east wall also had to be renewed. Scott's clerk of works at this time was Edwin Gwilt, who insisted that every new stone and joint should be an exact replica of what had been there before. Only in the tracery of certain windows was this rule of "conservative" restoration broken, Perpendicular-style tracery being replaced with Early English which, Scott argued, was more in harmony with the original thirteenth-century work. On the same principle he removed the late-sixteenth-century clerestory windows from the chancel, and built a pitched roof which the roof-scar on the east wall of the tower suggested was the original form.

Thus far, nobody appears to have disagreed with Scott, but there was considerable controversy over what he proposed to do with the south transept.   This part of the church seems to have been extensively damaged by the collapse of the spire in 1593, and it had been largely rebuilt in what Scott regarded as a very debased form of Perpendicular. Surviving drawings show that the transept had a flat roof with battlements, set at a much lower level than the nave and opposite transept. The parapet and cornice were so low that they intersected the flattened arch of a large six-light window with Perpendicular-style tracery.

Given its dilapidated condition and the "late and corrupt" style of its architecture, Scott proposed to "restore" the south transept to what the surviving evidence suggested was its original thirteenth-century form.   The line of the former pitched roof was deeply marked on the tower wall, while the south window and wall of the transept itself contained enough evidence to show that there had once been a triplet of very tall lancets separated externally by small buttresses, the bases of which were still *in situ*.

One of the principal parishioners of S. Mary's, and a subscriber to the restoration scheme, was Stafford banker Thomas Salt, whose brother-in-law, the Revd J.L. Petit, was an architectural historian soon to become well-known for his drawings and writing. (11) Having studied Scott's proposals for the south transept, Petit considered them to be a useless waste of money, and saw no advantage in replacing the existing window with triple lancets. Many subscribers agreed with him, and there followed a lengthy correspondence between Scott, Petit, Stevens and Coldwell over the propriety of proceeding with the scheme. (12)

For his part, Petit adopted what we would nowadays call a "conservationist" stance.   Look at any church or cathedral undergoing renovation at the present time. Regardless of current opinions as to the relative merits of architectural styles, where distinctive features such as doorways, windows and parapets have to be restored, then every effort is made to ensure that what goes in is a faithful replica of what is taken out. Scott, as we have seen, could be painstakingly conservative in replacing even the jointing of a wall exactly as he found it, but if he discovered that a certain feature had once been in the Ecclesiologists' beloved "Middle Pointed" style, then he considered it right and proper to "restore" it to what surviving evidence suggested its original form to have been. This was where Petit disagreed with him. Like most ancient churches, S. Mary's had undergone many additions and alterations to its original thirteenth-century form, and so inevitably it contained a variety of styles. Each one had its own story to tell about the building's development, and so every attempt should be made to preserve them - even those which latter-day architects such as Scott were denouncing as vile and worthless. "A period not very different from the time of the alterations he has condemned," argued Petit, "must have witnessed the erection of King's College Chapel, that of Eton College, the towers of S. Neots and Wrexham, and many other exquisite specimens".

Petit admitted that the late sixteenth-century transept at S. Mary's showed no great degree of excellence, dating as it did from a time when Gothic architecture was no longer in vogue. If the condition of the fabric required it to be rebuilt, then there was no need to adhere slavishly to existing details. He did however suggest that, instead of reverting to the almost obliterated design of the thirteenth century, Scott should preserve the Perpendicular character of the transept, and so fulfil the best intentions of the sixteenth-century restorers. To do more than this, Petit argued, would destroy the familiar character of the church as it had been known for generations, and lead people to dismiss the transept in particular as a "modern" invention.

Scott was not convinced. On the one hand, the existing form of the transept was in his view, "the very extreme of ugliness and barbarism ... the late insertions do not contain one feature which can render them valuable". On the other, his proposed restoration was "as nearly as possible in conformity with the original, and the design must have been a particularly fine one ... As therefore the late features are equally decayed with the early ones, I think it would be very bad judgment to perpetuate an unsightly innovation and to lose the opportunity of restoring a noble original".

It was finally agreed to refer the matter to the judgment of the Oxford Architectural Society and the Cambridge Camden Society, with almost predictable results. The Camden Society had already taken an interest in the schemes of its new convert: its co-founder, A.J.B. Beresford-Hope was among the subscribers to the restoration fund, and its journal, *The Ecclesiologist*, printed an article expressing approval of Scott's intended restoration. A sub-committee was set up, and in May 1842 Benjamin Webb himself communicated its view that, given the necessity of rebuilding the south transept, "it would be more advisable to return to its ancient form which appears at once beautiful, imposing, and appropriate, than to retain the bad workmanship of a debased age".

So Scott's plan went ahead, and it was vindicated in that, as the transept walls were taken down, much more of the original work came to light than he had expected to find. In the re-used masonry and rubble core of the sixteenth-century rebuilding were portions of the internal mouldings from the piers and arches of the original triplet, and the pieces of a quatrefoiled circular window from the former gable. Based as it was on extensive archaeological evidence, there is no doubt that Scott's new transept was an accurate reconstruction of what had been there before 1593, but a significant part of the church's later history was swept away in the process.

16 *South elevation of S. Mary's, 1842 (from Scott/Moffatt drawings in Staffs. County Record Office).*

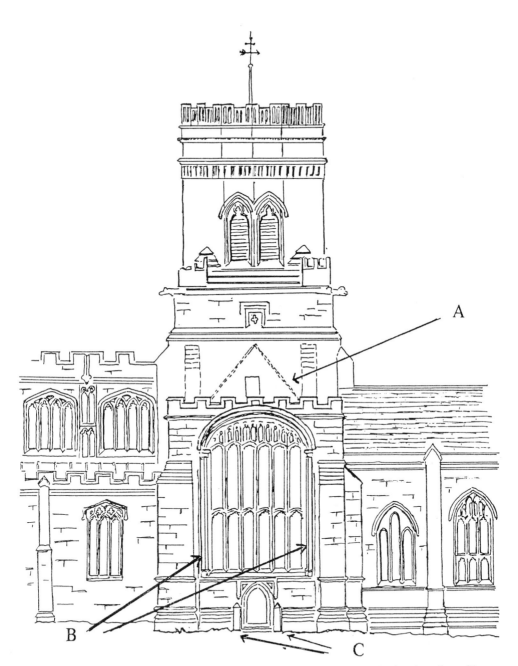

17 S. Mary's, Stafford: elevation of south transept and tower (1842) showing the evidence used by Scott to reconstruct the original form of the transept: A – roof-scar showing pitch of medieval roof; B – jambs of 13th-century lancets; C – bases of buttresses which had separated the original triplet.

18. *The south transept as reconstructed by Scott (from Masfen's* Views, *1852)*

19 View of S. Mary's from the south-east during the reconstruction of the south chancel aisle. From an original drawing by J. Buckler 1842 (William Salt Library, Stafford)

20   Drawing presented to the Revd. W.E. Coldwell by Scott and Moffatt showing the proposed restoration of S. Mary's, Stafford, 1842

21. S. Mary's from the south-west – John Masfen

22   S. Mary's: the nave, 1844 – John Masfen

23   S. Mary's: the north transept   -   John Masfen

24 S. Mary's: the south transept 1844 – John Masfen

25   S. Mary's: the chancel 1844   –   John Masfen

26   S. Mary's: the south chancel aisle   –   John Masfen

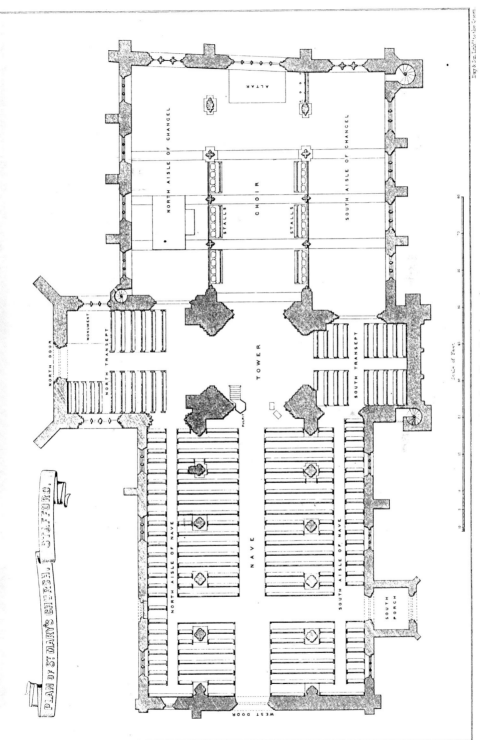

27 Plan of S. Mary's showing Scott's internal re-arrangements

28 S. Mary's, Stafford – the nave looking west following the re-ordering of the church in the 1960s and '70s. The nave altar stands close to where the parochial altar would have been in medieval times, and the organ has been moved back to its pre-1842 position, but at floor level.

29. The canopied sedilia at S. Mary's. Scott, influenced by Pugin, believed such furnishings to be essential to the proper celebration of the English Liturgy.

Scott's remaining plans for the exterior of S. Mary's were impeded by shortage of money. He built a new south porch, which many subscribers considered to be an unnecessary waste; but the money ran out before he could rebuild the spire which, oddly enough, nearly all of them wanted. Scott expressed regret that the north transept had to be left completely unrestored, and this may be the origin of the legend still persisting in Stafford that, given the necessary money, he would have done to the north transept what he had done to the south. The evidence suggests otherwise. In the first place, the north transept is an outstanding example of the early-fourteenth century "Middle pointed" which Pugin, Scott, and the Ecclesiologists alike extolled as the highest perfection of Gothic architecture. Secondly, Scott himself described the transept as "one of the most elaborate and beautiful parts of the church..... as fine a specimen as is often to be met with of the geometrical variety of the Decorated or Middle Pointed style," (13) and he proposed to do nothing more than repair it as it stood.

In the post-nineteenth century reaction against Victoriana much was said and written about Scott's "destructive" restorations. Even Basil Clarke's pioneer appreciation of the High Victorian period (1938) doubted if anyone would ever admire the works of Scott, "for there is nothing in particular in them to admire." (14) It is now possible to take a more balanced view, and it would seem, on balance, that Scott had much more in common with Mr. Petit than with the Ecclesiologists. Indeed, it is difficult to avoid the conclusion that his first flush of enthusiasm for the ideas of the Camden Society was cooled as a result of his altercations with Petit over S. Mary's. Certainly the Society became critical of his work, and in his *Plea for the Faithful Restoration of Ancient Churches* (1850) Scott argued along Petit's lines that restorations should be conservative in nature. "It is often preferable to retain reminiscences of the age of Elizabeth, or James, or the martyred Charles, rather than to sweep away, as is now the fashion, everything which dates later than the Reformation." He even ended his essay with "some appropriate lines" by Petit himself. Scott did not always take his own advice, but against his "destructive" restorations one must set others such as his careful conservative work at Salisbury and Houghton Conquest, and his determination to preserve the Baroque porch of S. Mary the Virgin in Oxford, which others would gleefully have swept away. It was as a memorial to Petit's brother-in-law, Thomas Salt, that Scott completed the restoration of Stafford's other ancient church - S. Chad's - in the early 1870s, scrupulously matching its existing features in the Norman style which the Ecclesiologists despised.

Had it not been for the chain of coincidences which brought together Scott, Stevens, Coldwell, Salt, Petit and Watts Russell in the common concern of restoring S. Mary's Stafford, the career of Gilbert Scott might have taken a different, and less distinguished, path. S. Mary's itself would no doubt be a less impressive building than it is today if dilapidation had been allowed to continue beyond the point at which less scrupulous architects, or more "advanced" Ecclesiologists, would have pressed for a much more radical solution. Thirty years later Scott admitted that too little actual old work had been preserved, and even expressed doubt as to whether he was right in his views about the controversial south transept. Nevertheless, he looked back on it as the best restoration carried out at that time, "nor have many since been in the main much better." (15) Pugin, who in the early 1840s was also working in North Staffordshire, visited S. Mary's several times, and he also designed the frontispiece for John Masfen's published prints of the completed restoration (16) which he pronounced to be "the best which has been effected in modern times". Scott could have desired no higher praise.

Notes to Chapter 1

1. Quoted by D. Morse-Boycott, *The Secret History of the Oxford Movement, 1933*, p. 12.

2. It needs to be said that the Diocese of Lichfield was more fortunate than many in having a succession of bishops at this time who were actively concerned with new church building, especially in the industrial areas: Ryder (1824-36), Butler (1836-9), and Bowman (1839-43). The Evangelical Bishop Ryder established a Diocesan Church Building Society which erected about 30 new churches and chapels by 1839. Though the architectural style of many of these buildings may have been imperfect, they fulfilled a crying practical need, and their internal arrangements perfectly reflected Anglican worship as it was then understood and practised. Pre-Tractarian Anglicanism required an auditorium, rather than a stage equipped for elaborate rituals.

3. George Gilbert Scott, *Personal and Professional Recollections*, 1879, p. 97.

4. John Masfen, *Views of the Church of S. Mary at Stafford*, 1852, p. 20. This contains Scott's own account of the restoration.

5. Scott, *Recollections*, p. 87.

6. *ibid.*, pp. 88-9.

7. *Victoria County History: Staffordshire*, vol. VI, p. 243.

8. John Masfen, *op. cit.*, p. 15.

9. In the transepts the pews faced inwards towards the tower crossing. The ecclesiologists raised some objection to this arrangement, but Scott said that the provision of such seating was the price he had to pay for getting rid of the galleries.

10. *Staffordshire Advertiser*, December 21st 1844.

11. J.L. Petit, *Remarks on Church Architecture*, 1841. Scott agreed with many of Petit's principles, and admired his sketches, but the Ecclesiologists had little sympathy with him.

12. Staffs. County Record Office MS D834/4/1/2.

13. John Masfen, *op. cit.*

14. Basil Clarke, *Church Builders of the Nineteenth Century*.

15. Scott, *Recollections*, pp. 99 & 100.

16. Masfen was a remarkably talented self-taught artist whose views of S. Mary's were done when he was only seventeen. He died aged nineteen and his drawings were published in 1852 with an introduction by Scott and a dedication to Jesse Watts Russell. In the north aisle of S. Mary's there is a memorial window to John Masfen, also designed by Pugin.

Pugin's visits to S. Mary's are recorded in the Staffordshire Advertiser report of 21st December 1844. There is a strange irony in the fact that Scott, who began his career as a designer of workhouses, should have received such high praise from Pugin, who, in *Contrasts* and elsewhere, was scathingly critical of the Victorian workhouse and all that it represented.

30. Augustus Welby Northmore Pugin. A portrait drawn from memory by Joseph Nash and used as the frontispiece to Benjamin Ferrey's **Recollections of A.N. Welby Pugin** *(1861)*

A.W.N. PUGIN AND S. GILES', CHEADLE

"An old English parish church, as originally used for the ancient worship, was one of the most beautiful and appropriate buildings that the mind of man could conceive," - Pugin.

While George Gilbert Scott was restoring the long-lost splendours of Stafford's Collegiate Church, his mentor, A.W.N. Pugin was realising his own ideal of an English parish church - S. Giles' Cheadle. Pugin is remembered as the designer of the sumptuous décor of the Palace of Westminster and the architect of cathedrals such as S. Barnabas' Nottingham and S. Chad's Birmingham, but it was the church at Cheadle and the castle and convent at Alton which he cited as his most successful buildings. Amid the many controversies, disappointments and personal losses which surrounded his short but brilliant career, S. Giles' was his great consolation, and when asked by a friend if there was any building with which this self-critical man was completely satisfied, he answered, "Yes, S. Giles' Cheadle; I don't think there is any fault there".

Yet S. Giles' is just one of several buildings which make northeast Staffordshire the prime area of the country in which to study and understand the mind of one who packed more into his sixteen years as a working architect and foremost exponent of the Gothic Revival than Scott did in forty. Pugin's work dominates this idyllic corner of the county. From the soaring spire of S. Giles' it is but four miles to Cotton, where Pugin's church and adjacent College of S. Wilfrid nestle in the vale below the village. A mile or so along the Farley road Alton Towers appears on the horizon, while beyond, on a precipitous rock overlooking the Churnet valley, stands Alton Castle, reminiscent of some Rhineland Schloss. All are monuments as much to the Catholic Revival as to the Gothic Revival, for in the mind of their architect the two were synonymous.

How does one explain this impressive concentration of Catholic Revival buildings in a small part of Staffordshire where Roman Catholicism was not especially strong? The answer lies with John Talbot, who, in 1827 succeeded his uncle as Earl of Shrewsbury and Waterford, Premier Earl of England. Like his predecessors, he was a devout Roman Catholic. The fifteenth earl had already begun to develop his Alton estate by laying out extensive pleasure-gardens on the site of an immense rabbit-warren ("he made the desert smile"), and converting a former hunting-lodge into a stately mansion. On inheriting the estate Earl John decided to abandon the family's Oxfordshire seat at Heythrop, make Alton Towers his principal residence, and complete his uncle's grandiose plans for it. In 1827 this may have been the limit of Lord Shrewsbury's intentions, but a few years later he met twenty-year-old Augustus Pugin and soon became infected with his growing enthusiasm for Gothic architecture. He also met another Catholic landowner, Ambrose Phillips of Grace Dieu in Leicestershire, who exhorted England's leading Catholic layman to assume a prominent role in the "Second Spring" of English Catholicism which followed the Catholic Emancipation Act of 1829. As a consequence, Shrewsbury's Staffordshire estates became the scene of building activity on a scale which Pevsner compares with that of King Ludwig II of Bavaria. (1) There was in fact a connection between the Shrewsburys and the Bavarian Wittelsbachs, but this was thirty years before Ludwig's time. (2) Moreover, whereas Ludwig sought to glorify royalty, Shrewsbury, Pugin and Phillips aimed at restoring the former glories of Catholic England. In Ludwig-land it was the king who went mad;

in Pugin-land it was the architect. So obsessed did Pugin become with Gothic architecture that towards the end of his life, it is said, he refused to eat puddings unless they were Gothic in shape, and even sculpted cheese and other foodstuffs into Gothic shapes. Of his third wife he wrote, "I have got a first-rate Gothic woman at last, who perfectly understands and delights in spires, chancels, screens, stained windows, brasses, vestments etc." It was as well, for within a short time of their marriage Jane Knill had to nurse him through the bouts of insanity and debilitating physical illness which led to his untimely death.

At the beginning of his career, however, Pugin was no more a church architect than Scott had been in his early years; nor was he, until 1835, a Roman Catholic. The only child of a refugee from the French Revolution, Augustus Charles Pugin, and his English wife Catherine Welby, A.W.N. Pugin was trained from childhood in his father's office as an artist, draughtsman and book-illustrator. A.C. Pugin had considerable self-taught skills in producing Gothic designs at a time when there was "a mania for building gentlemen's houses in imitation of castellated and monastic structures," (3) and this he passed on to his son to whom he entrusted King George IV's order for designing the furniture for Sir Jeffrey Wyattville's Gothic extensions to Windsor Castle.

It was as a furniture-designer that Pugin first encountered the Earl of Shrewsbury. In completing and decorating Alton Towers Earl John had to find a vast quantity of suitable furnishings and fittings. It is said that on a visit to a London dealer in 1832 he noticed some of the younger Pugin's drawings lying on a table and was so impressed with them that he asked to be introduced to the artist. What is certain is that within a few years Shrewsbury engaged Pugin to design and produce not only furnishings, but eventually to complete the structural alterations and additions that were to turn Alton Towers into one of the largest private houses in Europe.

Pugin later confessed that in the early 1830s he had little knowledge of the basic principles of Gothic architecture, and so fell into the same trap as many of his contemporaries who thought that a building or a piece of furniture could be made to look Gothic simply by the application of imitation Gothic embellishments, i.e. Gothick in the late eighteenth-century sense. Pugin did not, however, begin any structural work at Alton Towers until 1837, by which time he had discovered the basic principles of Gothic, namely that there should be no features which are not necessary for convenience, construction or propriety, and that all ornament should consist of enrichment of the essential construction of the building. This discovery came about as the result of his detailed studies of Salisbury Cathedral, carried out between 1833 and 1835. A widower at the age of twenty and bereft of both his parents by the time he was twenty-one, Pugin remarried and set up home in Salisbury where he settled down to the architectural and theological studies that were to change the whole course of his life - and the course of England's architectural history. For in saturating himself with the Gothic tradition of English church-building, Pugin the Protestant became painfully aware of a contrast between the spirit of those who had raised up such buildings in the Middle Ages and the spirit of those who had hastened their decay from the sixteenth century onwards. Built originally to proclaim the Catholic Faith, Salisbury Cathedral was now, in Pugin's mind, an empty shell, for in spite of its architectural grandeur God's glory no longer dwelt there.

By 1834 Pugin was convinced that Gothic architecture was the only true Christian architecture, and that "the Roman Catholic Church is the only true one, and the only one in which the grand and sublime style of Church architecture can ever be restored." (4) A year later he was received into the Roman Catholic Church. The reasons for his conversion were theological rather than aesthetic. As they were in the mid-1830s, Catholic ritual and Catholic churches offered nothing to one of Pugin's artistic perception. Here was another painful contrast: the rites for which noble buildings like Salisbury Cathedral had been raised were now being performed in perfunctory manner, with tawdry vestments and ornaments, in assembly-rooms which in Pugin's view were "inferior to many Wesleyan meeting-houses". The current Italian taste in ornaments, furnishings and vestments that was rife even in the private chapels of the wealthy were denounced as pure paganism, for its origin was not the Rome of the Popes but the Rome of the Caesars.

It is difficult to know which Pugin hated the most: the protestantism which had robbed England's ancient churches of their spirit, or the "paganism" which had robbed the Catholic liturgy of its proper architectural setting. Yet all around him, in England's medieval churches and cathedrals, were the clear signs of what had been there before the iconoclasts of the sixteenth and seventeenth centuries swept it away. For example, many of these buildings still contained pre-Reformation rood screens, separating the chancel from the nave, and though shorn of most of their medieval splendour, including the large crucifixes which were their principal *raison d'être*, they were to Pugin important evidence, and they formed the subject of one of his last publications, *A Treatise on Chancel Screens and Rood Lofts* (1851). Pugin's view was that, after four centuries of divorce, Catholic liturgy and Catholic (i.e. Gothic) architecture needed to be re-married in properly-designed and furnished churches. Once restored to its ancient setting, Catholicism would no longer be viewed suspiciously by Englishmen as something foreign and unfamiliar. Instead it would be seen to be as much a part of England as the medieval churches in which the True Faith had once been celebrated and taught. In Pugin's mind the eventual restoration of England to Catholicism and the restoration of truly Christian art and architecture were but two sides of the same coin. His theory of the service of art to religion was expounded in the very first lecture he gave at Oscott College on the subject of Christian art in 1837:

"The Mass, whether offered up in a garret, or a cathedral, is essentially the same sacrifice; yet, who will allow that, when surrounded by all the holy splendour of Catholic worship, these august mysteries appear ten times more overpowering and majestic? ... may we not then confidently hope that, while the senses are rapt in ecstasy, by the outward beauty of holiness, the divine truths will penetrate the soul thus prepared for their reception".

Convincing students was one thing, but it was quite another matter to persuade the Catholic hierarchy that the main obstacles to the advancement of the Catholic cause included the word "Roman" and the Italianate paraphernalia that went with it. The English Romanists had their long-established customs which they saw no particular reason for changing at the whim of a twenty-five-year-old upstart convert whose speech ridiculed and insulted them, and whose eccentric clothes - a sailor's jacket, loose pilot trousers, shapeless footwear and broad-brimmed hat - cut no ice with the clerics whom he harangued on what they should and should not be wearing at Mass. There was, for example, a long-running battle over rood screens which Pugin saw as essential to an English church, but which his opponents decried because they prevented a clear view of the altar and interfered with the proper performance of various Italian devotions to which they were attracted.

Pugin said that at the time of his conversion he knew not a single Catholic priest, let alone a member of the hierarchy. He did, however, come to know England's leading Catholic layman, and as the friendship between Pugin and Lord Shrewsbury grew, he was introduced to the many prominent clergy and laity whom the earl entertained at Alton Towers. Shrewsbury was captivated by the genius and impetuous enthusiasm of this extraordinary young man, but even he was dictated to over the design of his proposed new dining room at Alton: the earl must either accept Pugin's design in its entirety or have nothing at all. (5) It was the noble earl, not the junior architect, who had to give way. The result was a banqueting hall described many years later by King Edward VII as the finest room he had ever dined in. (6) It has a huge oriel window in the end wall, still containing heraldic stained glass designed by Pugin and executed by Hardmans of Birmingham. Other echoes of the splendour which once filled this great mansion are the two chimney-pieces carved with the Shrewsbury arms and motto, and the painted roof-timbers.

Pugin's other work at the Towers is not now easy to identify. When he arrived there in 1837 he was faced with a building on which a number of architects had worked since 1810, including James Wyatt (who died in 1813) and Uttoxeter-based Thomas Fradgley. Wyatt was the architect responsible for building the most famous Gothick fantasy of all time: Fonthill Abbey, dreamt up by the millionaire Samuel Beckford and started in 1796 on a hill not far from Salisbury. It may be no accident therefore that Alton Towers was first known as Alton Abbey. At Alton Wyatt repeated the axial plan of Fonthill: tall, narrow ranges linked by a central octagon reminiscent of a cathedral chapter house. The principal axis at the Towers is 460 feet long, running from the main entrance through the former Armoury to the octagon and the Talbot Gallery beyond. All this was in place when Pugin arrived on the scene in 1837, and much of it was "fake" Gothic of the kind that Pugin was to scorn in his later writings. The vaulting of the octagon roof was made of plaster rather than stone, so structurally it was a complete sham, but fairly typical of James Wyatt whom Pugin denounced as a "monster of architectural depravity". Much as he might have wished to start afresh and create something better, Pugin had to content himself with inserting the great Banqueting Hall into an existing range, building the south facade of the domestic block, finishing the internal décor, and remodelling and completing the chapel. Like the Banqueting Hall, the chapel is impressively high, but empty, the furnishings and even the wall-panelling having been disposed of long ago. Pugin's main surviving contribution here is the ceiling, richly coloured in blue, red and gold, and recently (1994) restored and illuminated by floodlighting.

While the buildings at Alton Towers were in progress, Lord Shrewsbury gave Pugin the chance to build a perfect example of a small parish church along medieval lines. Five miles south of Alton is the market-town of Uttoxeter where, in 1838 Gilbert Scott had that historic meeting with Thomas Stevens which led to his pioneering work at S. Mary's, Stafford. In the same town, and within a few months, Pugin began work on what he described as "the first Catholic structure erected in this country in accordance with the rules of ancient ecclesiastical architecture since the days of the pretended Reformation" - S. Marie's, Uttoxeter. (7) Thus it differed radically from what was then accepted practice in Catholic church building and furnishing. The architectural style was that of the early thirteenth century, and in design, furnishing and decoration it marked a clear reversion to the customs of English medieval Catholicism. One of the most remarkable things concerned the reservation of the Blessed Sacrament which, instead of being placed in an elaborate tabernacle on the altar, was housed according to medieval custom in a hanging pyx suspended above the altar. So startlingly different was S. Marie's from what Catholics were familiar with that, on hearing that vestments of the "Old English" style were to be worn instead of the "normal" Italianate ones, Bishop Baines, Vicar

*31   The Staffordshire seat of the Earls of Shrewsbury:
"Alton Abbey"   before its tranformation into "Alton
Towers".   Engraving by Jones, c 1820, published in
Neale's* **Views of Seats** *1829*

32   Alton Towers: steel engraving by H. Warren, c 1860

74

33   Alton Towers - the Banqueting Hall

75

34 A page from **Contrasts** *(1836) showing what Pugin describes as a "faithful picture of Protestant desecration and neglect": a defaced altar screen below which stands a "cheap ugly table" in place of a proper altar.*

35 "More suited to a fashionable boudoir than an altar for sacrifice". Pugin contrasts the "pagan" and "profance" neo-Classical furnishings of many Catholic churches.........

36. ....with the "true Catholic" (i.e. Gothic) altar which Pugin sought to revive. (from **Contrasts** *1836)*

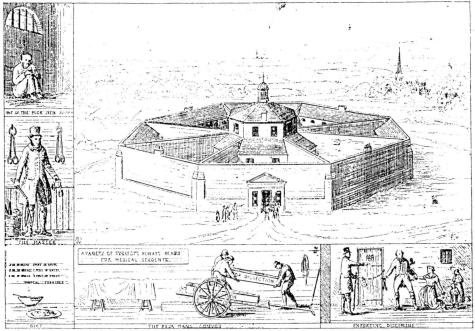

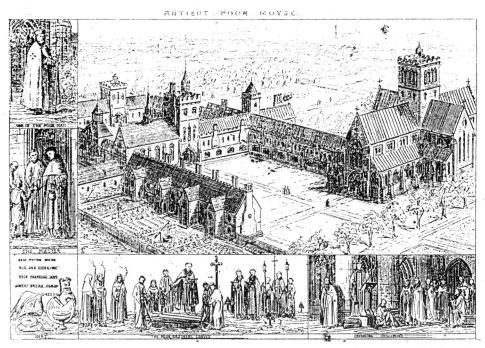

37 *The Gothic Revival had an important social content. Here Pugin contrasts the brutal treatment of paupers by the Protestant State under the 1834 Poor Law Amendment Act with the "venerable almshouse" of medieval England. S. John's Hospital at Alton represents Pugin's and Lord Shrewsbury's attempt to revive the Catholic almshouse along the lines illustrated in this engraving from the 1841 edition of* Contrasts

Apostolic of the Western District, refused to attend the opening ceremony.

At Uttoxeter Pugin was able to demonstrate another point, namely that the basic essentials of a Catholic church could be provided tastefully at modest cost. This was important, for although a few individual patrons like Lord Shrewsbury were wealthy, the English Catholic Church as a whole was not. S. Marie's, Uttoxeter was originally a very simple building of brick with a stone trim: a nave without aisles, a chancel carefully expressed by a lower roof level than that of the nave, and a bell-cote set over the western gable. It was more of an invention than a true revival, and after it was built Pugin did not believe it was truly Gothic, but in it he was stating an order of precedence in which the chancel and its fittings were of prime importance. (8) The Uttoxeter plan was repeated in other places, but all of these small and simple churches have subsequently been altered or enlarged.

It was Pugin's writings, more than his buildings, which earned him national fame (and notoriety) between 1836 and 1841. In 1836 he produced *Contrasts*, a series of etchings contrasting the noble Catholic architecture of the Middle Ages with its tasteless nineteenth-century counterparts. The accompanying text expounded Pugin's thesis that the Catholic mind had produced all that was praiseworthy in the arts, that Protestantism had destroyed true art as well as true religion, and that the current degraded state of the arts in England was the inevitable result of a lack of Catholic feeling. So scathing was the satire that no publisher would accept it, so Pugin had it printed and published at his own expense. *Contrasts* quickly ran to a second edition, and although it made enemies it also found many sympathisers inside and outside the Catholic Church. All the illustrations for this and for his other publications were done by Pugin himself. Not only was he a skilled draughtsman; he could also work under conditions that others would have found impossible. One set of etchings he completed while at sea in a stiff gale off Calais. "The motion of the sea makes no difference to me," he said to his incredulous publisher. He could also work extremely quickly. In 1842, having been invited by the Fellows of Balliol College, Oxford to submit designs for a considerable amount of rebuilding and extension, Pugin produced within a fortnight not only the usual detailed architectural drawings, but also large-scale perspectives in water-colour of the interiors and exteriors of all the proposed new buildings. In spite of their brilliance the plans were vetoed by the Master of Balliol, Dr. Jenkyns, who refused to employ a Catholic architect, particularly, one may assume, one whose writings were as "anti-establishment" as Pugin's.

Nevertheless, as we have already seen, Pugin's *Dublin Review* articles excited Gilbert Scott and the Anglican Ecclesiologists almost to fever-pitch, and lectures given to students at Oscott College (9) formed the nucleus of his most original and influential book, *The True Principles of Pointed or Christian Architecture* (1841). The Dublin Review article of the same year likewise formed a significant part of *The Present State of Ecclesiastical Architecture in England* in which Pugin set out a history of parish church building, the traditions associated with it, and his proposals for nineteenth-century church designs and furnishings. It was by parish churches, he believed, that the ancient Faith had been sustained and nourished; and so it would be by parish churches that England would return to that Faith, provided that they were recognisably Christian (i.e. Gothic) from the ground upwards. Included amongst the illustrations of parish churches which Pugin had designed for this purpose but not yet built were the projected designs for the one which was to occupy his best endeavours for six years and which he promised would be "a perfect revival of an English parish church of the time of Edward I" - S. Giles', Cheadle. Neither the woodcuts nor the promise equal the

38 Like a page from Pugin's **Contrasts** *– the two churches of S. Giles at Cheadle*

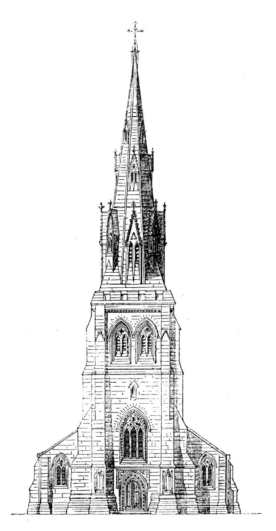

*39 Pugin's drawing of the tower and spire of S. Giles'
for his 1841 Dublin Review article.   Additions and
enlargements took place during the course of building.*

40 John Talbot, sixteenth Earl of Shrewsbury. Portrait by Julius Hamburger showing the chapel at Alton Towers in the background. (Reproduced by kind permission of Sandwell M.B.C.)

41 Alton Towers chapel - panelled ceiling by Pugin, restored 1994

84

42 *Alton Castle – perched on the edge of the Churnet valley like some Rhineland Schloss*

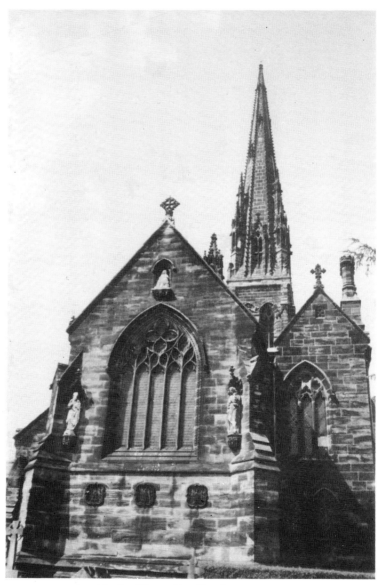

43 S. Giles', Cheadle, from the east

S. Giles', Cheadle: 44 The nave; 45 View through the elaborate brass screen into the Blessed Sacrament Chapel

46 S. Giles', Cheadle: the chancel arch and rood screen

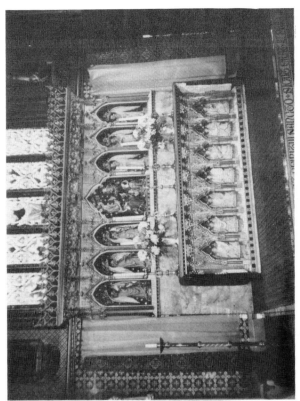

47 & 48 S. Giles', Cheadle: the chancel and high altar with figures carved by local sculptor Thomas Roddis

49 & 50   S. Giles', Cheadle: the Shrewsbury lions in evidence on and around the west doors

51 S. Giles', Cheadle: the north aisle. Drawing by J.L.Williams, **Illustrated London News,** *9th January 1847*

reality of S. Giles'. Planned originally as a simple parochial church, it grew, thanks to the architect's power of persuasion and the Earl of Shrewsbury's wealth, into a far more sumptuous building in which most of Pugin's ideas about church architecture and decoration were realised as nowhere else. It is, to use a modern-day turn of phrase, "a total Pugin experience".

Cheadle has two churches dedicated to S. Giles: J.P. Pritchett's Anglican S. Giles' begun in 1837 to replace its decayed medieval predecessor, and Pugin's Catholic S. Giles' begun just four years later. Placed side-by-side these two churches might well have come from a page of Pugin's *Contrasts*, for they give a striking illustration of the changes which took place over these years, thanks largely to Pugin, in the understanding and application of Gothic architecture. Pritchett's church is admittedly of the better kind of the so-called "Commissioners' Gothic", and its interior furnishings and decorations have been radically altered since the 1840s. When first opened, however, it had all the features which Pugin ridiculed: an embraced west tower, a box-like nave without a proper chancel, windows with incorrect forms of tracery, galleries on three sides, and a three-decker pulpit obscuring the altar. In other words, it was basically a preaching-house overlaid with a veneer of quasi-gothic ornament which would fool nobody. By contrast, Pugin's S. Giles' is revived Gothic in its totality, from its foundations to the raised forefinger of the graceful spire which seems to beckon its Anglican neighbour, "Come and see how it ought to be done!"

At S. Marie's, Uttoxeter Pugin had shown what could be achieved on a tight budget: cheap did not necessarily mean nasty. At Cheadle the £5,000 which Lord Shrewsbury had originally proposed for the building of a plain parish church was suddenly increased while work was actually in progress, so the character of the building changed from that illustrated in the *Dublin Review* article as it assumed a degree of grandeur and richness never previously thought of. Two months before the consecration in 1846 John Henry Newman wrote that it had already cost between £30,000 and £40,000, and though he was not particularly fond of Pugin or of Gothic Revival architecture, he described S. Giles' as the most splendid building he had ever seen.

A church, according to Pugin's *True Principles*, should express through its architecture and decoration the divine purpose for which it is intended, each part of the building clearly defined for its specific function, yet at the same time fully integrated. His reflection on the medieval glories of an English parish church serves also as an accurate description of S. Giles':

"What is more appropriate for the ancient worship than an old English parish church with its heaven-pointing spire - the beautiful and instructive emblem of a Christian's brightest hopes? How well-suited too, is the interior of such a church for the performance of Catholic rites - the spacious nave and aisles for the faithful ... the impressive doom or judgment pictured over the great chancel arch, the fretted screen and rood loft; the mystical separation between the sacrifice and the people ... the great altar rich in hangings, placed far from irreverent gaze, and all the long perspective terminating with the brilliant east window." (10)

This is precisely what Pugin created at Cheadle. Visible for miles around is the "heaven-pointing" tower and spire, surely one of the most perfect pieces of nineteenth-century Gothic Revival anywhere. (11) Taller and more ornate than originally shown in Pugin's drawings, the steeple dwarfs the nave and aisles. This was not the architect's intention, but one of the consequences of the sudden increase in funds which came about as the building work progressed. By 1844 it was too late to adjust the elevation of the church itself, so Pugin had to be content with enriching the interior and heightening and embellishing the spire. He was not altogether happy with the overall result. He later wrote, "Had we commenced on the same scale as we ended, a truly fine building might have been produced." (12) Self-criticism of this kind was typical of Pugin. Some years later his enthusiasm for what he himself had once called "perfect Cheadle" was quoted to Lord Shrewsbury, who simply smiled and said, "He won't say that now though; he abuses it as much as everything else that he has done".

Below S. Giles' steeple, each part of the building - nave, chancel, aisles, porch and sacristy - is clearly defined by distinct roof-levels, and an ornate bell-cote was built on the east gable of the nave so that the Sanctus could be rung to remind those passing by while Mass was in progress that the Holy Mysteries were being celebrated within. No doubt Pugin hoped they might kneel in the street, and make the sign of the Cross, as their medieval ancestors would have done. A Pugin church was nothing if not instructive.

Inside, S. Giles' has everything that one would expect from Pugin's vision of an English parish church that would, through the splendour and panoply of worship, instruct the faithful and draw in those as yet uncertain of their faith. Over the chancel arch is the "Doom" or representation of the Last Judgment, below which stands the fretted Rood Screen, emphasising a feature of English medieval churches that Pugin became obsessed with - the separation of the chancel from the nave and the protection of the altar from "irreverent gaze". (13) Other typically English features include the sedilia or stone seats set into the south wall of the chancel for priest, deacon and subdeacon at the High Mass. As if to underline the need for instructing even the clergy in how such refinements should be used, the seats are suitably labelled and decorated with the appropriate emblems - chalice and host, Gospel book, and wine and water cruets

- for priest, deacon and subdeacon respectively. On the opposite side is the Easter Sepulchre, set in an ogee arch glowing with gold and colours, and containing a painting of the entombment of Christ. No longer need the Mass be offered in "scrubby rooms called chapels where one urchin is frequently the only assistant at the holy sacrifice, which is offered up in a place and at an altar far more calculated to excite ridicule than devotion." (14) S. Giles' was indeed a model church, but to those steeped in the Roman tradition of Catholicism it was just too English, and Pugin was accused of trying to impress the Anglican Ritualists who were likewise taken with medieval English architecture and ceremonial.

Impress it certainly did. On January 9th 1847 - four months after S. Giles' was consecrated - the *Illustrated London News* carried a description of the interior which has probably never been bettered:

"When the church is lighted up for evening service the effect is gorgeous in the extreme; the gilded and diapered walls of the chancel glowing in the flood of yellow light of the tapers at the altar; the glistening gilded ceiling, forming a rich background to the lofty rood, with its pierced and elaborately-traceried screen; the coronae in the nave lighting up the painted and gilded pillars, their soft light fading away in the deep blue roof, whence the gilded stars sparkle with exquisite richness - form a picture, once seen, never forgotten".

Not only is S. Giles' an English church; it is very much a Staffordshire church in that local materials and local labour were used wherever possible in its construction. Lord Shrewsbury owned quarries not far from Cheadle, and from there came sandstone for the exterior and alabaster for the altars. The earl insisted that as much of the work as possible should be given to Cheadle men. Most of the carved stonework for the interior was done on site by a local sculptor, Thomas Roddis, for whom Pugin procured casts of medieval carvings to work from. He carved the pulpit from a single block of stone, and was responsible for the rich and varied mouldings of the pier capitals in the nave, and the alabaster high altar and reredos embellished with figures of angels. Although Pugin's tried and trusted friend George Myers was employed as principal builder, the clerk of works for the first few years was Mr Denny who had been associated with Pugin in the extensions at Alton Towers. Encaustic tiles for the floors and walls were manufactured in Stoke-on-Trent by another of the architect's friends, Herbert Minton, who at the same time was employing Gilbert Scott to build Holy Trinity Hartshill, a church which clearly reflects Pugin's influence.

Minton's tiles are but one feature of the interior decorations which make S. Giles' uniquely memorable. Archaeological evidence suggests that many medieval churches were ablaze with colour, not just in the form of stained-glass windows, but also decorations on walls and other surfaces. At Cheadle Pugin demonstrated in no uncertain terms his belief that this practice should be revived. So every inch is richly adorned with coloured decorations designed in the main by J.G. Crace, making the interior reminiscent of the medieval illuminated manuscripts from which Pugin adapted many of his ideas, or, in the words of Mr Trappes-Lomax, similar in effect to a piece of antique brocade. (15) Provision was made at S. Giles' for the Reservation of the Blessed Sacrament, not on the High Altar as was customary, nor in a hanging pyx as Pugin had done at Uttoxeter, but in a sumptuously-decorated side-chapel protected by elaborate screens of polished brass and wrought iron. This chapel made a particularly strong impression on the future Cardinal Newman, who could not help saying to himself, "This is the gate of heaven".

Pugin gave infinite care to every last detail, bringing together the wealth of knowledge of church decoration he had acquired from various sources - German, French and Flemish as well as English. The reredos in the Lady Chapel is a fifteenth century original bought by Pugin himself, part of his extensive collection of medieval religious artefacts. The rood-screen was inspired by his careful studies of surviving examples in Norfolk, and even the brass mountings on the altar-missal were faithful copies of ones he had seen on a book in Mainz cathedral. Pugin would have preferred silver for metalwork items like altar candlesticks, but Lord Shrewsbury began to urge economy, so apart from the sacred vessels themselves, all the metalwork is of brass or other base metal. Nevertheless, over a hundred items of Pugin-designed metalwork were produced for S. Giles' at the studio which he and his business partner John Hardman had opened in Birmingham. It cost Lord Shrewsbury £1280 - a huge sum in those days; it is the finest collection of Pugin's metalwork to be seen anywhere, and along with the sets of vestments which he also designed, it ensured that S. Giles' was singularly well-equipped for the task which the earl and the architect together had in mind for it. The church was consecrated on September 2nd 1846 by Bishop Walsh, amid solemn splendours never witnessed in Cheadle since before the Reformation.

S. Giles' is not the only Pugin building in Cheadle: he also designed the presbytery and the nearby school and convent of S. Joseph which formed a part of Lord Shrewsbury's scheme for a revival of Catholic institutions as well as churches. The earl was led into this scheme by his friend Ambrose Phillips who in 1835 started to build the first Cistercian abbey to be founded in England since the Middle Ages - Mount Saint Bernard in Leicestershire. Shrewsbury helped finance the project, Pugin designed the buildings, and Phillips pleaded with the earl to undertake a similar scheme in Staffordshire. There was a medieval precedent to guide him, for just south of Alton lie the impressive remains of Croxden abbey, a Cistercian foundation endowed in 1179 by one of Shrewsbury's ancestors, Bertram de

Verdun of Alton Castle. The earl, however, wanted something more practical than the mere revival of an enclosed order of monks. Instead he and Pugin proposed to build in Alton village "a perfect revival of a Catholic hospital of the old time, of which so many were seized and demolished by the sacriligious King Henry and his successors in church plunder". (16) It needs to be said that the challenge of Pugin to the England of his day was social as well as architectural. His *Contrasts* contained comment on attitudes towards the poor, for example the contrast between the venerable almshouse of the Middle Ages and the Victorian workhouse in which conditions were made deliberately unpleasant. Now, at Alton, he had the chance to make it a reality: what Catholic art and Catholic charity could do in caring for the poor and the infirm, as opposed to the penny-pinching and degrading treatment meted out in the grim workhouses created by the Poor Law Amendment Act. The result was an impressive complex of buildings on the opposite side of the Churnet valley to Alton Towers: the church and hospital of S. John the Baptist, and Alton Castle.

"Hospital" in its medieval sense did not signify a medical institution, but what we now might call "sheltered accommodation" for the elderly, the infirm, and the destitute who might otherwise be homeless. This practical attempt to re-create the medieval collegiate life which he admired so much excited Pugin enormously. Now shared by Benedictine monks and S. John's Junior School, the buildings at Alton consisted of "a chapel, school, lodging for the warden, common hall, kitchen, chambers and library for the six chaplains, lodgings for the poor brethren, and a residence for the schoolmaster". (17) The chapel also served as a parish church for the Catholic population of Alton who, until it was built, worshipped in the earl's private chapel at the Towers.

Beyond the hospital lies the ravine-like ditch and the remains of Bertram de Verdun's twelfth-century castle around which Pugin began to build the new Alton Castle in 1847. Perched on the edge of a precipice, this amazing composition rises four storeys high, with three towers and an apsidal chapel roofed in coloured and gilded tiles. The chapel is rib-vaulted in stone, and has tall, narrow windows with geometrical tracery. Though now (1994) empty of most of its furnishings, it is still, in the words of Sir Nikolaus Pevsner, "a room which inspires worship". The precise purpose for which the castle was built remains something of a mystery. It may have been intended as a residence for the earl's nephew and heir, Bertram, or to serve ultimately as a dower house for the countess. Still unfinished at the time of Pugin's (and Lord Shrewsbury's) death in 1852, it is nevertheless a key building of the architect's career, and indeed of the Gothic Revival as a whole. Gone is the fanciful "gothick" of the Towers; here is a solid, handsome building, truly Gothic from bedrock to the lead-covered spirelets and steeply-pitched chapel roof which make it an interesting composition from wherever one looks at it.

By the time that S. Giles' Cheadle was opened, the Catholic Revival had taken a new turn with the secession to Rome of John Henry Newman, Frederick Faber, and several other prominent members of the Anglican Oxford Movement. Their conversion had cost them their careers, and many Catholics viewed them with suspicion. Lord Shrewsbury saw that such men needed shelter and the opportunity to work out their future, and so he gave Cotton Hall, a fine mansion close to Alton Towers, to Faber and his Brothers of the Will of God. Newman joined them there, and among other former Anglican priests who came were Michael Watts Russell, second son of Jesse Watts Russell who had financed the restoration of S. Mary's at Stafford. The Brotherhood was eventually absorbed in the Birmingham Oratory, but not before Pugin and Shrewsbury had extended the buildings at Cotton. The most significant addition was the church of S. Wilfrid, which Pugin declared would be "the only perfect church in England", with an east window he could die for.

Pugin died at the age of forty on Holy Cross Day, September 14th, 1852. His physical and mental health had been failing for some time under the self-imposed burden of overwork, and there were times when he had to be confined to a mental hospital. His doctors told him that he had crammed a hundred years' work into twoscore: an understatement, for the bulk of his undertakings - eight books and two dozen smaller publications, over a hundred complete buildings, numerous restorations and furnishings, and a prolific output of church metalwork and vestments - were packed into the years 1838 to 1848. On top of all that, Pugin found time for three marriages and eight children, one or two unsuccessful courtships, a voluminous correspondence with friends, clients and patrons, all handwritten of course, and to operate a one-man lifeboat service from Ramsgate where he built his second family home, S. Augustine's Grange. (18) He loved the sea, and sailing was probably his only relaxation. His speed and accuracy as a draughtsman have already been noted. When asked why he did not do as many architects did, and employ a clerk to carry out the routine and mechanical aspects of his drawings, Pugin replied that any such clerk would be dead from overwork within a week. Instead he effectively sacrificed himself.

Lord Shrewsbury outlived him by only a few weeks, dying of malaria in Naples in October 1852. His body was brought back to England and buried in the church of S. John at Alton. (19) So ended a unique partnership between architect and patron which left an indelible mark on the architectural history of England. Outside Staffordshire Pugin often found himself cramped by insufficient funds, and infuriated by Catholics who did not share his enthusiasm for "Christian" art and architecture. Well might the Catholic hierarchy recoil in horror against one who vilified their most sacred buildings: "S. Peter's (Rome) is far more ugly than I expected... the Sistine Chapel is a melancholy room... The Vatican a hideous mass". Ironically, the people who paid most attention to Pugin's Gothic propaganda and visions of a holy England full of spires, stained glass, twinkling candles and incense-laden ritual were members of the Church of England. Thus Pugin's influence extended much further than he could ever have dreamed. Though he had only one pupil in the formal sense - John Hardman Powell - his ideas were taken up enthusiastically by contemporary and successive generations of architects, and his medieval ideal was popularised in the Great Exhibition of 1851. Concepts such as truth to materials, honesty of design and manufacture, and the integration of architecture and the decorative arts, were also a part of Pugin's "true principles", and they were keenly adopted by men such as William Morris and the founders of the Arts and Crafts Movement of the later nineteenth century.

Notes to Chapter 2

1. N. Pevsner, *Staffordshire*, p. 56.

2. Lord Shrewsbury's daughter Mary married Prince Frederick of Saxe-Altenburg and was made a princess under the style of Princess Talbot by the King of Bavaria (Ludwig II's grandfather).

3. B. Ferrey, *Recollections of A.N. Welby Pugin and his father Augustus Pugin, 1861*, p. 5. Alton Towers was originally known as "Alton Abbey" although there had never been a monastic foundation on the site. "Wetley Abbey" (1836) a few miles north of Cheadle falls into the same category, and here the cross and mitre were used in decoration; cf. also Jesse Watts Russell's gothicisation of Ilam Hall in the 1820s.

4. Letter to his friend, Mr. Osmond Senr. of Salisbury - Ferrey, *op. cit.*, p. 88.

5. "... If I am not enabled to exercise my judgment, and make use of my knowledge and experience ... I really must decline undertaking the alterations ... Nothing can be more dangerous than looking at prints of buildings, or trying to imitate bits of them: these architectural books are as bad as the Scriptures in the hands of Protestants. I am very unhappy about it; and as regards the hall, I have nailed my colours to the mast - a bay window, high open roof, two good fireplaces, a great sideboard, screen, minstrel gallery - all or none." (undated letter from Pugin to Lord Shrewsbury quoted by Ferrey, op. cit., pp. 119-120).

6. According to Pugin's grandson, S.P. Powell. M. Trappes-Lomax, *Pugin, A Medieval Victorian, 1932*, p. 117.

7. So Pugin wrote in the *Orthodox Journal*, 20th July 1839, p. 33. In referring to the Blessed Virgin, he preferred the ancient spelling, "Marie", to the more modern "Mary".

8. Phoebe Stanton, *Pugin*, 1971, pp. 42-43.

9. At the age of twenty-five Pugin was appointed Professor of Ecclesiastical Art and Antiquities at the Catholic Seminary at Oscott, at the request of Lord Shrewsbury (1837). In addition to lecturing to the theology students there he held Sunday afternoon classes for craftsmen from Hardmans, Birmingham, the firm which manufactured ecclesiastical metalwork for him. He also filled a museum at Oscott with church furnishings made to his designs, for the instruction of students in the proper conduct of the Liturgy.

10. *Contrasts*,p.49.

11. Pevsner, *Staffordshire*, p. 97. The tower and spire are 200 ft. high.

12. *Some Remarks on Articles which have recently appeared in the Rambler*, 1850, p. 9.

13. When showing an Anglican friend his rood screen in S. Barnabas' Nottingham, Pugin said, "Within is the holy of holies. The people remain outside. Never is the sanctuary entered by any save those in holy order". Then, to his horror, Bishop Wiseman appeared in the sanctuary, showing the screen to two ladies. Pugin retired to the nearest bench and burst into tears. M. Trappes-Lomax, *Pugin,* 1932, p. 222.

14. E.S. Purcell, *Life and Letters of Ambrose Phillips de Lisle*, 1900, vol. ii, p. 215.

15. Trappes-Lomax, *op. cit.,* p. 118.

16. *Dublin Review*, May 1841.

17. Pugin's own description in the 1841 *Dublin Review* article, later reprinted in *The Present State of Ecclesiastical Architecture in England*, 1843, pp. 92-5.

18. Pugin's first wife, Anne Garnett, died in childbirth a year after their marriage. In 1833 he married Louisa Burton and moved to Salisbury where he designed and built S. Marie's Grange, complete with private chapel, in the style of a small fifteenth-century manor-house. Later he moved to Ramsgate where he built a much more impressive residence, S. Augustine's Grange, and adjoining it is the church which served both as the Pugin family chapel and local parish church. Pugin was buried here in 1852.

19. Since Lord Shrewsbury died childless his estates and titles passed to his nephew and heir who also died without issue. The succession was then the subject of a lengthy legal battle which ended in the thwarting of attempts to keep the estate in Catholic hands. The inheritance finally went to a cadet branch of the family, the Chetwynd-Talbots of Ingestre. Since they were Anglicans the financial support formerly given to S. Giles' Cheadle and the Catholic institutions at Cheadle and Cotton ceased abruptly. In 1857 almost the entire contents of Alton Towers were sold by auction at an extraordinary sale in which it took thirty days to dispose of nearly 4,000 lots. The altar from the Towers Chapel is presently at S. Peter's, Bromsgrove.

52   George Edmund Street   (frontispiece from A.E. Street's **Memoir***, 1888)*

G.E. STREET AND ALL SAINTS' DENSTONE

"Who among preachers can hope to preach as the gifted artist does? It is not only that the sermons are in stones or on walls or canvas, but they are read and believed by generation after generation of the faithful" - G.E. Street.

Three miles from Alton castle is the village of Denstone, famous for its College, established in 1868 by the Revd Nathaniel Woodard as part of his scheme for making public-school education more widely available to people of modest means. The village also contains a church, vicarage and school designed in 1860-62 by G.E. Street for a patron who had very firm views on the Church's role in education, and the need to provide decent schools and attractive churches for the working classes. Complemented by a lych-gate and churchyard cross, Street's buildings at Denstone are more widely-spaced than Pugin's buildings at Alton, and so visually they do not form as coherent a group, but they are in their way just as important, and particularly the church of All Saints'. Here, concludes Pevsner, is young Street at his very best, and, according to the late Sir John Betjeman, Denstone was the architect's own favourite church.

Like Pugin before him, George Edmund Street (1824-1881) believed himself to be a man with a mission, but whereas Pugin regarded architecture as the handmaid of Roman Catholicism, Street was a High Church Anglican who aimed at restoring to the Church of England a rich heritage which had been either lost or obscured since the sixteenth century. "I am, I suppose, what you call a Ritualist, for I belong to the party which for twenty years has been striving with no small success to raise the whole tone of Church opinion and practice both in architecture, music, ritual and doctrine." (1) The party to which he refers was of course the Cambridge-based Ecclesiological Society which, like the Oxford-based Tractarians, believed that the Church of England was not the "invention" of Tudor monarchs and thus a tool of the State, but heir in direct line of the medieval English church whose origins went back at least as far as St. Augustine. As in matters of doctrine the Tractarians pointed to those parts of the Book of Common Prayer which appeared to encourage a Catholic view of the Sacraments and the priesthood, so the Ecclesiologists took their stand on the Ornaments Rubric which was inserted into the Prayer Book at the time of Elizabeth I. Although it had never been strictly enforced, the Rubric seemed to allow a wide range of church ornaments and vestments, and the mere fact of unfamiliarity did nothing to stifle the zeal of the Ecclesiologists in seeking to re-introduce into the Church of England a whole range of "equipment", and associated ritual, which had not been seen there for three hundred years. Just as Pugin's brand of medievalism upset the conservative Roman mind, so the reappearance of long-neglected ritual and ornament within the Anglican church incurred the opposition of many Protestant-minded bishops and lay-people who raised the cry of "No Popery!" Attempts to curb the advance of ritualism culminated in the 1874 Public Worship Regulation Act under which Anglo-Catholic clergy were prosecuted, and some actually imprisoned.

The Margaret Chapel, just off London's Oxford Street, was noted as early as the 1840s as a place of "advanced" ritual practices. In 1858 it was demolished, but some of its furnishings, including the organ and pulpit, are still in use at S. Luke's church at Sheen, in the Staffordshire Moorlands, for the patron of Sheen, A.J. Beresford Hope, was a leading Ecclesiologist and a worshipper at Margaret Street. On the site of the Margaret Chapel William Butterfield was commissioned by Beresford Hope and others to build what is often described as the Ecclesiologists "model" church - All Saints', Margaret Street. This church, more than any other, had a profound influence upon the architect G.E. Street, for he became an active member of All Saints', and in 1867 he was appointed as its Warden by the Revd Upton Richards. In this position he enthusiastically supported the introduction of Eucharistic vestments and the enrichment of the altar as the focal point of the church.

Though greatly influenced by his High Church convictions, Street's career in architecture went back to teenage days when he was encouraged by his eldest brother Thomas to accompany him on church-sketching tours in various parts of England. Instead of joining the family firm of solicitors, Street entered the office of Scott and Moffatt to train as an architect, and in 1849 set up his own practice. Other influences at work upon the young Street included the Gothic architecture of France, Belgium and northern Italy - the result of several sketching-tours - and he came firmly to believe that although Gothic was the most beautiful and most useful style of architecture, there was nothing to be gained by ignoring the existence of all Gothic forms other than English ones. In this respect he came close to Butterfield, whose churches - including All Saints', Margaret Street - often display a wealth of inlaid marble patterns and polychrome stone and brickwork inspired by continental examples. The sketching-tours were to prove useful in many ways, not least in teaching the young Street how to draw quickly and accurately. In this respect he was as impressive as Pugin. Norman Shaw later recalled how he and other of Street's pupils were awe-struck by one particular *tour de force*:

"... He told us one morning that he was just off to measure an old church - I think in Buckinghamshire - and he left by the ten o'clock train. About half past four he came back into the office for some drawing paper; he then retired into his own room, reappearing in about an hour's time with the whole church drawn carefully to scale, with his proposed additions to it ... all ready to ink in and finish. Surely this was a sufficiently good day's work! two journeys, a whole church measured, plotted to scale, and the new parts designed in about seven hours and a half." (2)

Street's early work in Staffordshire includes the restoration/rebuilding of S. Mary's, Colton (1850-52), S. Nicholas', Abbots Bromley (1852-5), S. Mary's, Blymhill (1856-9), and the new church of S. John, Hollington (1859-61). They contain most of the features characteristic of a Street church: a wall-like chancel screen constructed of variegated marbles and built exceedingly low so as not to obscure the altar, a circular pulpit inlaid with coloured stones and set well clear of the chancel arch, and the altar itself raised on a flight of steps and backed by a reredos of carved and inlaid marble and alabaster. All of these features were at their time strikingly novel, and would have contrasted sharply with the rather plain and colourless church interiors to which most people were accustomed.

Until 1862 Denstone had no church, and its only school was a Dame School where a very basic education was provided for the children of local farm labourers. Members of this small rural community worshipped at one or other of the neighbouring village churches: Alton, Ellastone and Norbury. The provision of a church, vicarage and school was the work of Thomas Percival Heywood of nearby Dove Leys House. He was one of fifteen children born to Sir Benjamin Heywood from whom, as eldest son, he eventually inherited the baronetcy. The Heywoods were a Manchester banking family, and deeply involved in education which they believed should be universally available. Sir Benjamin was for all practical purposes the founder of the Mechanics' Institution, and its President for many years, while also taking a leading role in the reform of the famous Manchester Grammar School. In matters of religion the Heywoods were Nonconformists, and Sir Benjamin was a Unitarian, but he eventually joined the Church of England, and his sons became Tractarians.

Percival Heywood's choice of thirty-six-years-old G.E. Street to design his buildings at Denstone may have been influenced by the work which Street had already done in Staffordshire villages, and also by his brother, the Revd Henry Heywood, Vicar of Swinton near Manchester, who was a keen Ecclesiologist. Ample funds were available for Street to design and build an original composition, constructed entirely in stone from the nearby Hollington quarries. Percival Heywood himself laid the foundation stone of the church at a service presided over by Bishop Lonsdale of Lichfield on December 29th 1860, and on July 24th 1862 the Bishop returned to dedicate the completed building under the title of All Saints'. In his sermon, Bishop Lonsdale laid stress on the fact that it was "especially a church for the poor, and that every seat was free and unappropriated, and was intended to remain so for ever." (3) This was a reference to the system, obtaining in very many churches, of "pew rents" whereby those who were able to afford it could reserve their own seats, often to the exclusion of the poor. It was a practice which Street absolutely loathed, for he believed that the Church should be the leveller of social classes. At All Saints' Margaret Street he fought hard to ensure that every single seat there was kept free, against those who feared the financial consequences of the abolition of pew-rents. Percival Heywood agreed with him, and was proud to point out that the system he operated as churchwarden at Denstone guaranteed free seats for all and healthy finances, (4) and this may have helped to convince any remaining doubters at Margaret Street that a system which worked well in a country church could also be applied successfully in London.

53 All Saints', Margaret Street, London, by William Butterfield (1859); the model church of the Ecclesiological Movement, where Street was churchwarden

54 & 55 All Saints', Denstone: nave and chancel, south side

56a Inside the chancel at Denstone

56 All Saints', Denstone: north side.

57 All Saints', Denstone – the marble and alabaster reredos

As if to emphasise the indelible nature of these arrangements at Denstone, the words, "Every seat in this church is free", are cut in stone just inside the door, and the provision of individual chairs, instead of the usual open benches or pews, was a quite deliberate ploy (again adapted from All Saints', Margaret Street) to make it impossible for two people to appropriate the space for three. Conspicuous by its very absence is anything remotely resembling a "Squire's Pew", or a separate entrance for the "family of the hall" such as one sees in many a manorial church. The Heywoods took pot-luck with their seats, just like anyone else. It goes almost without saying that the common practice of "going up" for Communion in a strict pecking-order according to one's social status would hardly have been countenanced at Denstone.

The segregation of the sexes was something else which Street insisted upon at his London church, where as late as the 1960s the men sat on one side of the nave and the women on the other, except in the very back rows behind the Wardens' seats. The object of the exercise was to stop the usurpation of men's seats by women, and thus encourage more men to come to church by making special provision for them. It worked at Margaret Street, where the attendance of men greatly increased; while at Denstone Percival Heywood, doubtless under the architect's influence, insisted that the men should occupy the south side of the nave, and the women the north where the seats were more widely-spaced to accommodate their voluminous mid-Victorian attire! A reason for Street's particular fondness for Denstone must surely lie in the fact that Percival Heywood was completely at one with the architect, not just in matters of building and design, but also in the continuing business of how the church and its services should be run.

The plan of All Saints' Denstone is very simple. It has a nave without aisles, a porch on the south side, a chancel and a bell-turret, each element delineated by a different roof-level as Pugin said it should be done. It is what Street does with these basic features that makes Denstone so interesting and endearing. Instead of the chancel being lower than the nave as was normal in English churches, it is much taller, a fact emphasised by the downward slope of the ground at the east end, and the height of the windows. Instead of the usual square-ended English chancel, Denstone has a French-style polygonal apse. Pugin had already done a similar thing at Alton Castle chapel, and given the close proximity of Alton it is possible that Street was influenced by it, although he gave the windows the robust plate tracery which he preferred to the more slender and intricate bar tracery favoured by Pugin. Instead of a bell-cote set on a gable, or even a western bell-tower, a round turret with quatrefoil bell-openings and a conical top is set at the junction of the nave and chancel, but the turret does not start at ground level. It grows out of the oblong, groin-vaulted passage to the organ chamber and vestry on the north side, and one enters it via an exterior staircase.

The fabric is of rough-faced grey Hollington stone, with smooth horizontal bands of contrasting pink. The window-arches are likewise built of alternate blocks of pink and grey: a mild form of polychromy. Butterfield was to take it to excess in some of his buildings, with bold patterns blazoned in variously-coloured brick, but Street uses it here in a very gentle manner. The same scheme is repeated on the inside: irregular coursing in undressed grey stone with horizontal bands of smooth pink, and on the inside we also find the use of other stones such as Derbyshire marble, Isle of Man limestone, and alabaster.

The church is full of surprises. On the south side of the nave are three broad windows, all of three lights, but each having a different tracery pattern in the head. One might expect to see a similar arrangement on the north side, but it is in fact totally different. There is first of all a large sexfoiled window which gives light to the font, then four simple lancets which on the outside look small, but which on the inside have deep splays at the sides and very deep slopes below. The guide-leaflet to All Saints' asks, "Is there any other nave with so great a difference between its south and north windows?" The answer is that the Staffordshire architect Thomas Trubshaw produced a comparable piece of architectural "roguery" at S. James', Salt, just outside Stafford, and as early as 1840-42, but it is not quite so dramatic. (5)

The texts cut into the wall between the window-splays, and the hanging brass coronae and other light-fittings designed by Street add dignity to the nave. The fittings - including some highly original wall-sconces - are now electrified, but originally they would have held candles. There was also an efficient heating system. It was important to Street and Heywood that the people's part of the church should be both dignified and comfortable.

The surprises continue into the chancel which, in addition to the tall, two-light windows, has small quatrefoils placed high up, rather like clerestories. On the inside, however, these are fronted by rectangular recesses separated by shafts of black marble, looking for all the world like a mini-tribune or triforium, but hopelessly - and delightfully - out-of-place. The apse windows are marble-shafted too, as is the broad and lofty chancel arch.

Under the chancel arch is a low screen of stone and marble, of the "Margaret Street" type. Instead of being equipped with the usual gates, however, it is surmounted by polished brass tubes containing telescopic sections which can be drawn out to meet in the middle. The altar itself stands clear of the east wall, on the chord of the apse, and it is backed by a sculpted reredos of alabaster and inlaid marble. The centre panel represents the Crucifixion, with S. John, the

Blessed Virgin Mary and S. Mary Magdalene, while the side panels carry diapered groundwork which has been painted and gilded. Other features necessary for the correct performance of the Liturgy included a trefoiled sedilia for the officiating clergy, and a piscina for the ritual washing of the sacred vessels. Sumptuous altar-frontals were provided, along with brass altar-candlesticks and other furnishings, for the altar and its immediate surroundings were to be the focal point, as Street and the Ecclesiologists believed should be the case in every church.

The floor of the chancel is composed of various coloured marbles and Minton's tiles. The pulpit, tucked away at the junction of the chancel screen and south wall, is of the circular type we expect of Street, decorated with crosses and bosses of inlaid marble, lush foliage, and twisted "barley-sugar" colonettes. Thomas Earp did much of Street's woodcarving and stonecarving, and he was responsible for the font at Denstone. It is square in plan, supported by green Galloway marble columns. The alabaster bowl has angels at the corners, holding upturned jars to symbolise the four Rivers of Paradise. The style of the figures derives from Niccola and Giovanni Pisano, a father-and-son partnership of thirteenth-century Italian sculptors whose work Street admired and which greatly influenced his own use of sculptured and inlaid marble.

The Consecration Service took place on Thursday July 24th 1862, and was conducted by Bishop Lonsdale assisted by thirty clergy including the Revd J. Cockerham, curate of Norbury, who was to be Denstone's first vicar. Choirs from neighbouring churches led the singing, which included "several appropriate hymns and psalms in the truly Gregorian style". Between the morning and afternoon services luncheon was provided for all at the expense of Percival Heywood, and a marquee was pitched at the side of the schoolroom to help cope with the 400 people who attended. All is carefully recorded by the pen of an observer whose description of the consecration of the churchyard is particularly eloquent:

" ... Near the entrance to the new church stands a lofty and beautiful churchyard cross. On the steps of this the venerable Bishop took his stand, the clergy and choirs, in their surplices, being grouped around him. The clouds had dispersed and the sun shone bright upon the new church in the immediate foreground; in the distance rose the Weaver Hills; all around was the rich scenery of the valley of the Churnet, and the woods of Alton; the trees and shrubs and turf were still sparkling from the shower which had passed. The gentry of the neighbourhood and the parishioners of Denstone were gathered in silent, reverent, throng, while the solemn prayer of consecration of the churchyard, in which many of them would have at last to sleep, was said ..." (6)

Denstone rapidly established a reputation for fine music and a stately liturgy. Many people were particularly delighted that plainsong chants were used for the Psalms - another mark of the Catholic Revival. In fact the Street-Heywood partnership produced at All Saints' exactly the kind of "Anglo-Catholic watering-place" that the Butterfield-Beresford Hope partnership had envisaged in the moorland village of Sheen. Denstone had one big advantage, and that was communications. The church and its associated buildings fronted a new road which linked the village with the towns of Cheadle and Uttoxeter, while a branch of the North Staffordshire Railway brought in people from further afield. And come to Denstone they did, for there was much to marvel at. On the first anniversary of the Consecration the preacher was none other than the Revd Alexander Heriot Mackonochie, vicar of S. Alban's Holborn who brought with him several of his choristers to augment the singing. S. Alban's was one of London's leading Anglo-Catholic churches, and Fr. Mackonochie was one of the most celebrated of the "martyrs of ritualism". In and out of the courts for some sixteen years on charges of "illegal" practices which included the use of vestments, altar-candles and incense, Mackonochie was eventually to be suspended from office at S. Alban's, and virtually forced to resign. In his sermon at Denstone, Mackonochie contrasted the happy circumstances of a country parish with those of his own sphere of work in London where "in the almost incredibly small space of a few hundred square yards eight thousand people are closely packed in every phase of wretchedness". It was nevertheless through the building and endowing of churches like Denstone and S. Alban's Holborn that "the means of grace are brought home to Christian people in all their beauty and integrity." (7) Mackonochie was noted as much for his pastoral work in the slums as for his ritualism, for in his mind the two went together, offering visions of splendour to those whose daily lives were dull, and Christian charity to those in desperate need.

In August 1880 the people of S. John's church at Miles Platting decided to make Denstone the destination of their summer outing, and they came by train from Manchester for a special service in the church and a picnic tea. Accompanying them was their Rector, the Revd S.F. Green, a friend of the Heywoods who had served his curacy under Percival's brother at Swinton, and who had already been to Denstone as visiting preacher at the 1868 Dedication Festival. In 1879 Fr. Green had been prosecuted for "ritualism" under the Public Worship Regulation Act, and the case was to have yet more serious consequences. In welcoming the visitors to Denstone the Revd H. Meynell (curate) assured them of the sympathy and support of his people over the stand which Fr. Green and his congregation were making "for Christ's truth and Christian liberty". The sympathy and support were soon to be needed. Fr. Green had refused to pay the costs awarded against him by the Court, so he was declared to be in contempt and his personal property was seized. In March 1881 he was committed to Lancaster Gaol, where he was to stay for over eighteen months, and his household goods were sold by public auction. Fr. Meynell and the churchwardens of Denstone petitioned for his release, and in a letter to the editor of the *Manchester Guardian* stated that his imprisonment and the seizure of his goods was "a disgrace to our age and country, and an insult to Almighty God in the person of His minister." (8)

There appear to have been no controversies over matters of ritual at Denstone. Heywood, Street and Meynell were after all establishing a new church, rather than changing accepted practice in an existing one, and unlike some of the more "advanced" ritualists, they kept strictly to the rubrics of the Book of Common Prayer. The pattern of the services was nevertheless uncommon at the time, especially for a rural parish. The three Sunday services, Mattins, Eucharist, and Evensong, were all fully choral, and provision was made for weekday worship too. A service sheet for Easter 1871 is still extant, and shows that the Tallis responses were used at Mattins and Evensong, together with anthems and plainsong psalms, while at the Eucharist the choir's repertoire included the *Missa de Angelis* as well as settings by Merbecke and Helmore. Lent, Holy Week and Easter were scrupulously observed with a host of special services and addresses, while the Dedication Festival in July and the Patronal Festival in November were frequently covered by detailed reports in the local Press and attracted visitors from afar. (9) The only known controversy was the one which Fr. Meynell had with a local Methodist minister over the "Camp Meetings" held in the vicinity of Denstone by the Primitive Methodists. According to Meynell these meetings attracted undesirable hangers-on who got drunk and then disturbed the neighbourhood by roaring out bawdy songs to the tunes of well-known hymns!

Street went on to do more work for the Heywood family. In 1869 he rebuilt the eighteenth-century church at Swinton for Sir Percival's brother. He is perhaps best remembered as the designer of the Royal Courts of Justice in the Strand, but four-fifths of his work was for the Church. Denstone must rank as one of his most successful projects, not least because he was working for a patron who was keen to establish a church which, in matters of practice as well as architecture, fully accorded with Street's own views. "This is an unusually able and original design", concludes *The Ecclesiologist*, "under circumstances where novelty was scarcely to be expected". This lovely little gem of a church, so full of surprises, attracted attention and admiration from way beyond the borders of Staffordshire, and it marks a significant stage in the architectural and religious history of England.

Notes to Chapter 3

1. A.E. Street, *Memoir of George Edmund Street, R.A.,* 1888, p. 67.

2. *ibid.,* p. 284.

3. *All Saints' Scrapbook,* pp. 33-35. This folio-sized book, kept at Denstone Vicarage, contains a variety of items connected with the history of the church from 1860 to 1894; hand-written eye-witness accounts, cuttings from local papers, service-sheets, photographs etc., and is therefore the prime source of information for the early days of All Saints'.

4. Letter to "The Church of the People", *All Saints' Scrapbook,* p. 39.

5. The aisleless nave at Salt has five small windows on the north side. On the south there appears to be just one window of seven lights, but inside the seven lights are divided into 1 + 5 + 1 by two corbelled-out columns supporting roof-trusses.

6. *All Saints' Scrapbook,* pp. 27 & 29.

7. *ibid.,* pp. 37 & 39.

8. *ibid.,* p. 143.

9. *ibid.,* p. 89. In a press-cutting (source unknown) on this page a contrast is drawn between the Easter services at Denstone and the next parish of Norbury: "The congregation (at Norbury) numbered between 30 and 40, and there were whole blocks of vacant pews. The parish clerk was the only occupant of the chancel. On one of the walls of the church was an illuminated inscription, "Unto you is born this day a Saviour which is Christ the Lord" (!) ... The musical parts of the service were simply execrable. The wretched playing (piano-wise) on a small and somewhat indifferent organ went far to convert the singing into a burlesque. Certainly the contrast, as regards the service and attendance with the neighbouring church of Denstone, with a smaller population and a much smaller endowment, was very striking and suggestive".

58 George Frederick Bodley. Photograph reproduced by kind permission of the British Architectural Library, RIBA, London

G.F. BODLEY AND THE CHURCH OF THE HOLY ANGELS, HOAR CROSS.

"Bodley can nowhere be better judged than here; loving care could not be further expended" - H.S. Goodhart-Rendel.

As an active member of the English Church Union and of its central Council, G.E. Street would have come into regular contact with its President, Charles Lindley Wood, son and heir of the first Viscount Halifax. Charles Wood was to Anglican Catholicism what Lord Shrewsbury had been to Roman Catholicism: an energetic and dedicated advocate of the cause he believed in, and a generous patron of its architecture and art. Both men lent aristocratic respectability to ideas and practices that were frowned upon by the hierarchies of their respective churches. Charles Wood lived much longer than Shrewsbury however, dying in 1934 at the age of ninety-five, and his earnest desire to see Anglicans and Roman Catholics re-united led him into the famous conversations with Cardinal Mercier at Malines just after the First World War. His sister Emily shared his Anglo-Catholic outlook, and in 1872 she engaged George Frederick Bodley to build a church which would be a perfect expression of their religious beliefs - the Church of the Holy Angels at Hoar Cross.

The little village of Hoar Cross lies a mile or so off the road from Abbots Bromley to Burton-on-Trent, and until 1874 it had no church at all. Approaching the village along a leafy lane and past the gates of the Hall, visitors today are suddenly faced with a building of almost cathedral-like proportions, and many wonder why such a tiny village should possess so grand a church. The answer lies in Emily's unwavering devotion and considerable wealth, and the commitment which she and her brother had to the Anglo-Catholic cause.

Much to the *chagrin* of his parents, Charles Wood was drawn to "High Church" ideas and practices during his undergraduate days at Oxford in the late 1850s. Partly through the influence of his father, Charles became Groom of the Bedchamber to the Prince of Wales, but when in 1868 he accepted the presidency of the English Church Union it became painfully apparent that his new duties might prove incompatible with his position in the Royal Household. Queen Victoria's low opinion of ritualistic practices was no secret, and in her eyes the Union must have been a most objectionable society because of its support of ritualist clergy in their defiance of the courts and its encouragement of "illegal" practices. It may sound strange to modern ears that what went on in church was regulated by Parliament, but such was the nature of the Church of England, much as the High Church party detested it. To begin with, the Prince of Wales was much less concerned than his mother. "If ever I become religious, I shall be of Charley Wood's religion", he is supposed to have said on one occasion. (1) Later on, the Prince and Princess often attended Evensong at All Saints' Margaret Street, where they would have come into close contact with "Charley Wood's religion". In the short term, however, Charles had to choose between the Court and the Church Union, and he chose the latter. Many years later, when he became Viscount Halifax, he changed the family motto from *Perseverando* to *I Like My Choice*, in allusion to his own choice between his work for the Church and his position in the household of the Prince of Wales. (2)

Emily Charlotte Wood was not only Charles' sister, but his favourite companion and confidante from childhood through to her death in 1904, so it is hardly surprising that she came to share his religious convictions. At the age of twenty-three Emily married

Hugo Meynell Ingram, a man almost twenty years older than she was. Hugo was well-connected: through his grandmother Frances Ingram he was soon to inherit Temple Newsam, a fine Elizabethan/Jacobean house near Leeds, and through his Meynell grandfather the Staffordshire estate of Hoar Cross. Charles approved of the relationship, and declared that even if Meynell Ingram had not a penny, it would make no difference so long as Emily liked him.

After their marriage in the autumn of 1863 Hugo and Emily went to live at Cross Hayes, not far from the Old Hall at Hoar Cross and the famous Meynell Hunt Kennels. Their married life was short, but exceedingly happy, and Hugo was a great favourite with all the Woods. On the death of his father in 1869 he succeeded to the family estates, and Hoar Cross Hall was rebuilt at this time in the style of the Ingram family home at Temple Newsam. Hugo did not live in it for long. In February 1870 he was injured in a hunting accident and died in May of the following year, presumably as a result of the accident. Hoar Cross was in the parish of S. Peter Yoxall, so Hugo was buried there among his Meynell ancestors.

It was a tragic blow. Emily had no children to comfort her, and her sisters-in-law, as well as being much older than her, resented the fact that Hugo had willed her the whole of his estate. Her energies were, however, very quickly absorbed in the building of a church at Hoar Cross in Hugo's memory. Work began early in 1872. By January 1874 it was possible to hold services in the nave, and on April 22nd 1876 the church was dedicated by the Bishop of Lichfield, George Augustus Selwyn, under the title of The Holy Angels. A few days later the body of Hugo Meynell Ingram was removed from Yoxall to a splendid tomb and chantry chapel prepared for it in the new church. That might have been the end of the story but for Emily's determination to make Hoar Cross the finest possible expression of the Anglo-Catholic Revival. The remaining twenty-eight years of her life were filled with schemes to extend and enrich the building, until, in December 1904, she was finally laid to rest by the side of her husband.

Few architects are told by their patrons that cost is immaterial, but when George Frederick Bodley was commissioned to design and build Hoar Cross church he had a virtually unlimited budget to work with. Even Lord Shrewsbury had felt it necessary to tighten the purse-strings a little as Pugin's ambitions at S. Giles' Cheadle began to soar, but Bodley felt no such constraints while working for Emily Meynell Ingram. As Mary Meynell later wrote, "Indeed, perhaps nothing is more worthy of note in the building and decoration of the church than the way in which Mrs Meynell Ingram and Mr Bodley never rested till each part and each detail were made as perfect as art and skill could make them ... Foundress and architect were at one ... and each fully recognised the other's genius and ability." (3) Such was the confidence and mutual trust between foundress and architect that the work was carried on without a formal contract, supervised by Bodley's local Clerk of Works, Mr. Peed.

Bodley's career as an architect began in 1854 in the office of George Gilbert Scott where he served a five-year apprenticeship. Subsequently he reacted against Scott's brand of Gothic and was much attracted to the works of Ruskin and the architecture of Butterfield and Street, both of whom he knew well. Consequently much of Bodley's early work shows their influence, notably the use of inlaid marbles, malachite and lapis lazuli, plate tracery for windows, and polychrome brick; much of this inspired by French and Italian buildings in brick and marble. He had an impeccable sense of colour and great talent for decorative design, and was the first architect to employ William Morris for the interior decoration of walls and ceilings. The churches of S. Michael & All Angels, Brighton (1858-63) and S. Martin Scarborough (1861-63) are among the best examples of "early Bodleian". By 1863 Bodley was reverting to the English, early-Decorated, forms of Gothic preferred by Pugin, and when he built All Saints' Cambridge (1863-70) and S. John's Tue Brook, Liverpool (1868-70) *The Ecclesiologist* noted with some satisfaction that "Mr Bodley has restricted himself to pure English forms", and observed that "the time for reaction from exclusively French or Italian types has at length arrived." (4) Then, in 1870-76, came the two churches for which Bodley is most renowned; S. Augustine's at Pendlebury, and The Holy Angels, Hoar Cross.

Both Pendlebury and Hoar Cross are masterly, but strikingly different. Pendlebury was financed to the tune of £50,000 by Edward Stanley Heywood, brother to Percival Heywood who engaged Street to build All Saints' Denstone. Inspired by the architecture of the cathedral at Albi, it is externally quite severe, depending almost entirely on structure for effect, with nave and chancel all under one long roof - a scheme which impressed Norman Shaw and influenced his church designs. Bodley planned a detached tower at the south-west corner, linked to the nave only by an archway, but it was never built. Nevertheless Pevsner considers Pendlebury to be one of the English churches of all time: "Its sheer brick exterior and the majestic *sursum* of its interior have never been surpassed in Victorian church building". At Pendlebury Bodley set out to create something new within the Gothic idiom, but at Hoar Cross he took as it were a step back to show what perfection was obtainable within the rubrics of fourteenth-century English architecture and decoration. Pevsner concludes, "How one man in one quinquennium of his life could have done both, believed in both, remains a mystery".

It remains less of a mystery when one considers the influences that were at work upon Bodley at Hoar Cross. There was his new associate, Thomas Garner, whose contribution to the interior design of the Meynell church was considerable. There was also Canon Frederick Sutton, a man experienced in a wide range of ecclesiastical crafts, including the designing of organ cases. His association with Bodley dates from the building of Hoar Cross. Finally there was Mrs Meynell Ingram herself, a lady with quite definite ideas of what she wanted, and who had no hesitation in ordering alterations as the building progressed. Furthermore, even after the church was supposedly finished in 1876, Bodley was brought back time and again to make further additions and modifications.

As originally planned, the church consisted of an aisled nave of two bays, a central tower, transepts and chancel, built of sandstone from quarries at Alton and Runcorn. No sooner was it finished than Emily had the west end pulled down and the nave lengthened by one bay to improve the proportions. The nave is dark, even on sunny days, as there is no clerestory and the windows are filled with stained glass by Burlison and Grylls, a firm which at this time Bodley used in preference to William Morris & Co.: a pity, comments Pevsner, for although there may be nothing wrong with Burlison & Grylls glass, "one is never tempted to look at it intensely, or twice". The nave, with its wooden, wagon-type roof, is, however, only a preparation for the chancel, from which it is separated by an intricately-carved rood-screen of the kind that Pugin would have loved. Beyond lie the crossing and chancel, both rib-vaulted, and the chancel rising to a greater height than the nave. Here the light floods in through large windows, illuminating a wealth of stone-carving such as is seen in no other Bodley church. Richly-decorated as are his churches at Tue Brook (Liverpool) and Cambridge, the ornament there is principally two-dimensional, making great use of colour on flat surfaces. Such schemes were, after all, less expensive than masses of carved and sculpted stonework. At Hoar Cross money was no object, and architect and patron were equally determined to create a late fourteenth-century interior more perfect than the fourteenth century could ever have produced. So the chancel walls are covered with statuary under richly-carved canopies, or standing in tiers on moulded brackets, and embellished with vine-scrolls, leaves and flowers - "wedding-cake Gothic" as some would call it - designed principally by Garner. Much of the actual carving was done by the Lichfield firm of Bridgeman and Sons, and the subject-matter - angels, archangels, apostles, bishops and martyrs - reflects the dedication of the building, and was intended also as a visible reminder of the presence around the altar of "angels, archangels, and all the company of heaven".

In the chancel the use of colour is more or less restricted to the glass of the windows, and to Frederick Sutton's elaborate organ-case on the north side. Parts of the organ itself came from Bangor cathedral. The focal point is, of course, the altar and its reredos consisting of two tiers of carved stone angels standing under pinnacled and crocketed canopies. Even the spaces between the figures are filled with pierced and traceried stonework, and as one might expect, the sanctuary is equipped with a stone sedilia for the officiating clergy at High Mass, and a piscina for the washing of the sacred vessels, all under elaborate canopies. There is no variegated marble as favoured by the younger Bodley, nor masses of Minton's brightly-coloured tiles as favoured by Pugin and Scott. All is three-dimensional natural stone, and the floor - redesigned on the instructions of the foundress after the consecration - is of black-and-white squares, lozenges, and heraldic patterns.

On the south side of the chancel is the church's principal *raison d'être*, the chantry chapel containing the tomb of Hugo Francis Meynell Ingram. The tomb lies under an ogee canopy of carved and pierced stonework, and consists of a tomb-chest with recumbent effigy sculpted in alabaster. He wears the uniform of the

Staffordshire Yeomanry, which he commanded, and, as one might expect, there is a Meynell foxhound at his feet. To the right, under the corresponding archway between the chantry chapel and the adjacent All Souls' Chapel, lies the tomb of Emily Meynell Ingram, also in the form of a tomb-chest with recumbent effigy in alabaster. Nearby is a monument to Emily's brother Frederick, whose devotion to the church was hardly less than her own, and who died in 1910. Others involved in the founding of the church are commemorated elsewhere. The likeness of Bishop Selwyn who conducted the consecration service is to be found in the statue of S. Chad overlooking the churchyard on the north side; Bodley appears outside the south transept in the guise of S. Basil, while Robert Bridgeman who carved many of the statues is commemorated in the narthex. He died in 1918. Likenesses of two prominent figures in the Tractarian Movement are recorded in the west window, where Dr. Pusey is portrayed as S. Thomas Aquinas, and in the north transept window where one of the most celebrated of the Victorian "martyrs of ritualism" - the saintly Bishop Edward King - is depicted as S. Hugh of Lincoln. This window also commemorates Canon Frederick Sutton.

Later additions to the fabric of the church comprised the Lady Chapel on the north side (1891), All Souls' Chapel (1900), and the narthex or ante-chamber at the west end of the nave (1906). The latter was designed by Bodley and carried out after his death by Cecil Hare. The provision of a narthex was allegedly suggested by Bodley himself after visiting the church one day and finding the main doors locked. It is said that it had been closed on the orders of the Bishop of Lichfield, who was attempting to curb High Church practices, and that Bodley was so annoyed that he built on the narthex from which the public could at least gaze into the church through a wrought iron screen. This story is almost certainly apocryphal, since none of the Bishops of Lichfield at this time was particularly anti-ritualist, and some were positively friendly towards the Meynell Ingrams. We do know, however, that Emily was very worried by the "Kensitites", an extreme Protestant body which went around the country interrupting services they disapproved of, and wrecking the interiors of Anglo-Catholic churches. On hearing rumours of a possible Kensitite attack on Hoar Cross, she instructed her four gamekeepers to sit by the church door during the Sunday service and to carry off troublemakers to a ducking in a nearby slimy pond. She added that she would pay any fines incurred! (5) The Kensitites never came, but the narthex with its wrought iron screen would afford protection if ever they did, while enabling visitors to view the church at times when it had to be kept locked for reasons of security. It may come as a surprise that such measures were needed in an age we imagine to have been less violent and more God-fearing than our own, but instructions given to clergy at this time on the care of churches often included precautions against thieves and miscreants. (6)

Hoar Cross Church contained a growing number of religious works of art lavished upon it by the foundress. If on her travels abroad Emily saw something that she thought would look well in her church she would attempt to buy it, or have it reproduced. The superbly-carved Stations of the Cross are a case in point. On a visit to Antwerp she was so impressed by the Stations in one of the great churches there that she engaged two local woodcarvers, Boeck and De Wint, to make a similar set. Originally the carvings were unadorned, but later on Emily had them painted and gilded by a special process she discovered after seeing the fine statues in the Marienkirche in Danzig (Gdánsk). First of all the figure is painted in colours, and completely overlaid with gold leaf. Then with a sharp instrument the gold is scratched off, creating elaborate diapered patterns as the colours underneath are revealed.

59 Church of the Holy Angels, Hoar Cross

60 Hoar Cross: the tomb of Hugo Meynell Ingram

61   Hoar Cross: the nave

62   Hoar Cross: the rood

63   Hoar Cross: the chancel

64   Hoar Cross: chancel north side: organ case by Frederick Sutton

65 *Hoar Cross: one of the set of Stations of the Cross by Boeck and de Wint*

Among the fine embroideries and vestments at Hoar Cross there is an antique chasuble of tapestry work which Emily acquired from the little church of Porto Fino on the Italian Riviera. There was a local tradition that it had been given to the church by Pope Gregory XI as a token of his gratitude for the hospitality he received while sheltering there from a storm which, in November 1376, interrupted his voyage from Rome to Avignon. It was probably this story, as well as the beauty of the vestment itself, which made Emily determined to acquire it for her church, so back it came.

Much as Emily loved her church, and lavished a fortune upon it, she believed - as Pugin and Lord Shrewsbury had done - that Catholic Christianity had an important social dimension. In her case it took the form of the Home of the Good Shepherd which she established in 1888 just outside the village, and which was later taken over by the Church of England Children's Society as S. Michael's House. Children from there were trained as altar-servers and choristers. There is evidence of a strong musical tradition at Hoar Cross, and it is said that a man who could sing well would stand a better chance of getting a job on the Meynell estate than one who couldn't.

"What did all of this cost?" is a question often asked by visitors to Hoar Cross. Emily made sure that no one would ever be able to give an accurate answer, and to her it was unimportant. No accounts or other paperwork relating to the building and adornment of the church are known to exist, and this would seem to confirm the story that Emily destroyed them all before she died in 1904. As for Bodley, he lived on for another two years, and among his last pieces of work was S. Chad's church in the nearby town of Burton-on-Trent, built at the expense (£38,000) of the first Lord Burton, of Bass Brewery fame. Begun in 1903 and completed after Bodley's death, it has a free-standing tower attached to the church only by a rib-vaulted corridor, i.e. an adaptation of his unexecuted scheme for a tower at Pendlebury; indeed the upper stages of the tower are taken directly from the Pendlebury drawings. S. Chad's may well be the best building in Burton, but Bodley's *chef d'oeuvre*, according to Goodhart-Rendel, is quite definitely Hoar Cross: "Bodley can nowhere be better judged than here; loving care could not be further expended. All the coloured glazing, the tombs, the fittings perfectly harmonious in the aristocratic, scholarly, mock-Gothic that is in a style of its own, and a remarkable one." (7)

The last word should perhaps be spoken by Mary Meynell, who thus concludes her guide-book written in 1922:

"And now I have told the Church's story and bid my readers farewell. In the silence and the soft dim light of the gathering darkness I kneel once more, and over my heart and mind come far-off memories crowding round.

I seem to see once more the old familiar faces and figures passing down the aisles. I see the gorgeous banners, the Cross uplifted high; I hear the soft tones of the organ and the children's ringing voices. I see the censer swinging wide, and those well-known tenors pass me, and the basses thunder by.

I see the sanctuary in its beauty with the Altar and its offering. I hear the solemn, 'Holy, Holy, Holy', wafted through the choir.

And then I turn to where a figure, silent, kneels apart in prayer. She is praying - can we doubt it? - for the church she gave here to God's glory."

1. J.G. Lockhart, *Charles Lindley Wood, Viscount Halifax,* 1935, vol. 1 p. 104.

2. *ibid.*, p. 214.

3. Mary Meynell, *The Church of the Holy Angels, Hoar Cross,* (Guide-book produced in 1922 and reprinted in 1959), p.13. Mary was the wife of Emily's younger brother, Frederick Lindley Wood, who took the name of Meynell.

4. David Verey, *"George Frederick Bodley", Seven Victorian Architects,* (ed. J. Fawcett), 1976, p. 89.

5. Lockhart, *op. cit.*, p. 218.

6. e.g. Percy Dearmer, *The Parson's Handbook,* (1899) argues that churches should not be kept locked during the day. Valuable items can be kept out of sight, alms-boxes made secure, and stewards recruited to keep an eye on visitors (pp. 52-55).

7. *The Goodhart-Rendel Index of Victorian Churches,* - National Monuments Record.

66 *Richard Norman Shaw: photograph by R.W.*
Robinson, reproduced by kind permission of the
National Portrait Gallery

RICHARD NORMAN SHAW AND ALL SAINTS' LEEK.

"The architects of this generation must make the future for themselves and knock at the door of Art until they are admitted" - R.N. Shaw.

On September 21st 1852 the body of A.W.N. Pugin was laid to rest in his church of S. Augustine, Ramsgate. Among those present at the funeral was a twenty-one-year-old student of architecture, Richard Norman Shaw, one of a new generation of British architects who acknowledged their debt to Pugin. Shaw was to develop his own ideas of what a church should be, and in 1885 work began on what is considered to be his best piece of church building - All Saints' Leek - barely ten miles distant from Pugin's own masterpiece at Cheadle. By a strange coincidence it was on the thirty-fifth anniversary of Pugin's funeral - September 21st 1887 - that Shaw carried out his final inspection of All Saints' and declared it to be "the best and most satisfactory piece of work I have ever had done".

Those who travel into Leek along the A520 Cheadle Road will catch a first glimpse of the squat tower of All Saints' before ascending the hill known as Compton, and will see something very different from Pugin's S. Giles'. Gothic it may be, but whereas Pugin and his followers visualised a church as a series of compartments, each with its distinct liturgical function, Shaw followed G.F. Bodley's example at Pendlebury by trying to create internal and external unity. The roof levels of nave and chancel are equal, and the broad, spacious interior is free of any visual impediment between congregation and altar. Pugin believed in tall chancel screens to protect the altar from "irreverent gaze" and to create an air of mystery, but Shaw applied the Tractarian principle - inherited no doubt from G.E. Street - that the altar should be visible from all parts of the building. All Saints' is therefore an "open-plan" church, with the kind of minimal chancel screen favoured by Street: a very low wall with gates, and without any superstructure. In matters of furnishings and internal decoration too there is much that is different from other Gothic Revival buildings of the period. Yet through conscious integration of of architecture and visual arts, All Saints' perfectly expresses Pugin's passionate convictions that arts and crafts are as important as architecture, and that they nurture each other. It is therefore the proper church on which to judge Norman Shaw as an ecclesiastical architect, and his clearest personal statement of the age-old belief that originality should derive from tradition. (1)

Leek in the nineteenth century was an expanding textile-manufacturing town. Its ancient parish church - S. Edward's - had galleries inserted in the 1830s to cope with increasing numbers. Then, in 1867, its chancel was rebuilt in Tractarian fashion by G.E. Street. On the east of the town rises the impressive tower of S. Luke's, a large church built by F & H Francis in 1848. The history of All Saints' begins with a dual-purpose school-church built at Compton in 1863 and served by a succession of curates from S. Luke's. This building still survives as a warehouse. Christ Church Compton, as it was called, was twice enlarged, but by the 1880s it was inadequate for the purposes of Sunday worship. The 385 sittings were usually fully occupied, and there were two celebrations of the Holy Communion besides Morning and Evening Prayer, and the Sunday School. The site for a new church, on the opposite corner of Compton and Southbank Street, had been acquired in about 1872, but it was not until 1885 that sufficient funds were available to start building. Even then it was uncertain if the whole church as designed by Shaw could be completed. (2)

The great families of Leek at this time included the Challinors, the Sleighs and the Wardles, all inter-related, and High Church by religious persuasion. Their business was in the silk mills and dyeworks for which Leek had become famous. The Challinor family had been major contributors to the extension of S. Luke's church in the 1870s, and it was Joseph Challinor who came forward with £3,500 towards the estimated cost of £10,000 for All Saints', his late brother John having given half the land for the site. Hugh Sleigh, who paid for the altarpiece and chancel decorations, was another major contributor, and grants were available from the Diocesan Building Society and the Incorporated Building Society, the latter, however, being conditional upon the whole church being completed.

Though not directly involved in the building of All Saints', the Wardles deserve mention as patrons of church restoration and ecclesiastical art. Thomas Wardle was a warden at nearby Cheddleton church, and he was also a friend of William Morris, which accounts no doubt for the abundance of William Morris glass and other decorations at Cheddleton which was restored by Gilbert Scott Jnr. in 1863-4. Scott employed as his local architect Edgar Wood, who built Christ Church, Compton, at the same time. Mrs Elizabeth Wardle was a founder-member of the Leek Embroidery Society, for which fine silks were produced at the Wardle mills. The main work of the Society was church embroidery, magnificent examples of which are to be seen in all the Leek churches, and indeed much further afield. (3)

The architect Richard Norman Shaw (1831-1912) had been a pupil of G.E. Street before setting up his own London office with his friend W.E. Nesfield in 1863, an arrangement which lasted until

Nesfield gave up his practice in 1880. Shaw was tall, thin, and distinguished-looking, quick of mind, suave and persuasive with his clients, and generous to his clerks. (4) His office became a school which attracted a large number of pupils and assistants, making it probably the strongest force in English architecture by the turn of the century. Among Shaw's pupils and assistants were Gerald Horsley and William Richard Lethaby, both of whom were involved in the design and furnishing of All Saints' Leek. Lethaby later wrote, "Shaw was not only gifted, but he was a delightful man. To work with him was all pride and pleasure and in a dozen years of work and play I never saw him irritated; he was amazingly generous and loved to praise us when he could." (5) It was his custom to go round the drawing-boards after the staff had gone home, and leave witty and beautifully-written notes and comments, which the men would find when returning to work the next day.

The catalogue of Shaw's executed projects includes two hundred complete buildings, of which only sixteen were churches. Among his best-known secular buildings are the great Northumbrian mansion, "Cragside" (1869-1883), Leyswood House, Sussex (1866-71), and London's New Scotland Yard (1887-90). Staffordshire has very few Norman Shaw buildings, and all of them are in Leek and the neighbouring village of Meerbrook. It was through the Sleigh family that Shaw rebuilt S. Matthew's church at Meerbrook between 1868 and 1873, the chancel being paid for by the last of another great local family, Elisabeth Condlyffe. He also designed two altar frontals for it, and some other items of needlework. In Leek itself Shaw designed a large private house for Hugh Sleigh: Spout Hall, 66-68 S. Edward Street, built between 1871 and 1873. Of stone with mullioned windows, projecting half-timbering, and large brick chimneys, Spout Hall is typical of Shaw's "Old English" houses. Later he came to favour the "Queen Anne" style, and it was this which had a profound effect upon William Sugden and William

Larner Sugden, the father-and-son partnership responsible for designing so many of Leek's public and private buildings in the last quarter of the nineteenth century. In Condlyffe Road, and within sight of Sugden's Gothic cemetery chapels, stand the Condlyffe Almshouses, built through the munificence of Elisabeth Condlyffe. They consist of two blocks of houses, built in "Old English" style with high gables and big chimneys, and approached through a handsome arch of brick and sandstone. Given Shaw's established connection with Miss Condlyffe, and the fact that Hugh Sleigh was one of Elizabeth's trustees (she died in 1878), it is more than likely that Shaw designed these almshouses too. (6)

Shaw's church at Meerbrook is an attractive building in a charming setting. He gave it the central tower with pyramid roof characteristic of many of his churches, and it reflects the influence of Street in the use of "Early English" motifs and a clearly-defined chancel. Yet he was already thinking of ways to coordinate nave and chancel, and was much influenced by G.F. Bodley's great church at Pendlebury where all is brought together under one roof. This inspired Shaw to abandon the Early English style in favour of a highly personal form of Perpendicular, with the simplest of mouldings, broad arches, and long, low profiles on the outside. S. Margaret's Ilkley (1875-77) was Shaw's first attempt to express these ideas; All Saints' Leek was to be his most successful.

Friday 26th June 1885, "Today I sign the contract for building All Saints' Church, Compton. May God in His great wisdom and mercy help me to complete the same to His Glory, my honour and everybody's satisfaction. Amen".

So begins a unique commentary on the building of a great church, written into three pocket-sized diaries by James Heath of Endon, who was given the contract for the building of All Saints'.

(7) A day-by-day, almost stone-by-stone, account of progress on the site from the signing of the contract to the consecration of the church in July 1887, is to be found in Heath's diaries, which also give glimpses of some of the forty or so men who worked for him, and an insight into the character of the master builder himself.

Thirty-six years old in 1885, James was brother to the "Moorland Poet", George Heath, who had died some years previously and lies buried in Horton churchyard. Though reared as a Methodist, James had found a new spiritual home in the Church of England, and specifically at S. Luke's Endon under the Revd J. Badnall whose preaching he greatly admired, and who appears to have recruited him as a Sunday School Teacher. Heath writes with all the zeal of a convert:

Sunday 23rd May 1886, "Morning school and church, Revd J. Badnall preacher. Afternoon school and afterwards to my brother William's for tea and then to Endon Wesleyan Chapel for the Sunday School Sermons, but I cannot enjoy their service like the grand old Church of England Service after all".

Family affairs also find a place in the builder's diary:

Saturday 27th February 1886, "I go to John Glover's at Burslem and buy a piano for the use of my children. May they be led to stay at home and keep from bad companions."

Wednesday 14th April 1886, "Mrs Heath ... is much shocked and astonished to find her sister Sarah and her husband falling out to the extent of blows on his side. I must say she is very aggravating with her tongue, but good in all other points. If they would only go down on their knees and pray for help, all would be well with them. God help them to do so, for their comfort and souls' sake. Amen."

SPOUT HALL, ST. EDWARD STREET, LEEK.
. ARCHITECT: R·N· SHAW 1871-3.

*67 Spout Hall, St. Edward Street, Leek, from a drawing in the Leek Public Library.
The windows no longer have leaded lights and the finials on the gables have gone.*

68   S. Matthew's church, Meerbook, by R.N. Shaw 1868-74

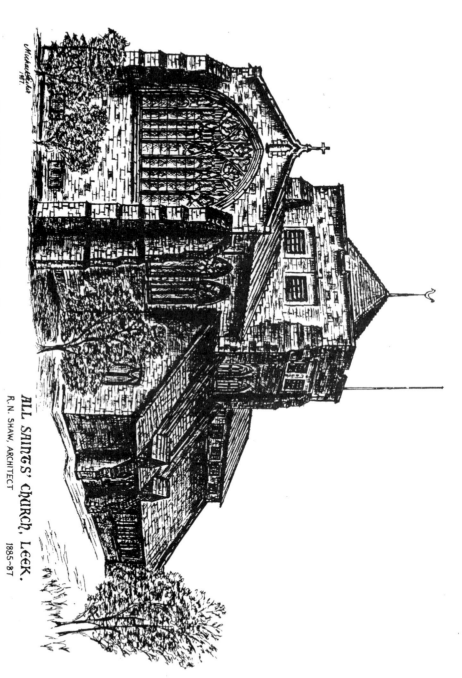

69   All Saints', Leek, from the north-east

ALL SAINTS' CHURCH, LEEK.
R. N. SHAW, ARCHITECT   1885~87

70   *All Saints', Leek – for comparison with S. Margaret's, Ilkley, below*

71   *S. Margaret's, Ilkley, by R.N. Shaw 1875-77*

72 All Saints', Leek – the nave under construction, 1886

154

73 The spacious interior of All Saints', Leek

74 All Saints', Leek – reredos by W.R. Lethaby and F.Hamilton Jackson

75 & 76 All Saints', Leek – details of chancel ceiling
and wall decorations
by Gerald Horsley

77   Gerald Horsley's painting of the Annunciation in
the Lady Chapel at All Saints', Leek

78 & 79 Furnishings by W.R. Lethaby at All Saints', Leek: the font and the pulpit

159

80 In the spirit of the Arts and Crafts Movement at All Saints' – one of a set of Stations of the Cross by Leek wood-carver J. Owen, 1991

81   A final flowering of the Gothic Revival in the
Staffordshire Moorlands - S. Chad's, Longsdon, by
Gerald Horsley, 1903-5, clearly showing the influence
of Norman Shaw at All Saints', Leek

All Saints' church was the most ambitious Leek building within living memory, and the overall responsibility entrusted to James Heath for executing the designs of one of Britain's most famous architects sometimes made him feel ill. He was, however, totally committed to his work, and he demanded high standards of his workmen. No swearing was allowed on the site, on pain of instant dismissal. (8) Two men were in fact sacked; a sawyer because of hard drinking, "which leaves us very awkwardly placed for sawn stone," and a mason, George Blunt, for "spending too long at the closet, so he goes". Another mason, George Rhead, was taken into custody for deserting his wife and children, while a W. Brown left to go and work on the Roman Catholic Church of S. Mary which was being built at Compton at the same time as All Saints'.

The site for All Saints' had been acquired in the 1870s, so it was by accident rather than design that Shaw was faced with an almost identical situation to the one he had cleverly resolved at S. Margaret's, Ilkley: a strong downward slope at the east end. He tackled it in exactly the same way, namely by providing a large vaulted undercroft containing vestries and a boiler-room to bring the east end up to the level of the nave. It also adds great interest to exterior views of the church. Seen from the north-west it looks low and broad, yet from the south-east angle it appears almost to double in height.

Exactly how much of the nave would be built was still uncertain when work commenced. Shaw disliked building by stages, and Heath was also anxious for the Committee to make a decision so that he could plan ahead. It was not however until February 1886 that sufficient funds were available to enable the Committee to accept Heath's contract for the completion of the nave at a cost of £1,983. Well might Shaw have envied Bodley's virtually unlimited budget at Hoar Cross; but by concentrating on broad open spaces, and by keeping architectural decoration simple, he was able to create buildings which could accommodate three or four times as many people as the Meynell church - as indeed Ilkley and Leek needed to do - at much less cost. Yet there is nothing cheap-looking about a Norman Shaw church. Considerable care was taken over the selection of the right building materials, and in James Heath the architect had the advantage of a local contractor who was thoroughly familiar with the geology and the quarries of the Leek area. Local materials were to be used throughout: rock-faced Kniveden stone for the walling, red Hollington sandstone for the windows and arches, tough Roach stone for the bases, weatherings and string mouldings, and the lovely pink sandstone from Ladderedge for the piers and copings. While cutting a roadway on the south side of the site, Heath came across a large quantity of sand which could be mixed with local limes to make suitable mortar, and trial walls were built before a start was made on the church itself. (9) As a consequence, All Saints' displays an interesting combination of the colours and textures of local materials worked by local craftsmen - a matter of great importance to the emergent Arts and Crafts movement which was being led at this time by some of Shaw's pupils and assistants.

The foundation stone of All Saints' was laid on July 25th (S. James' Day) 1885 by Mrs. J. Cruso, using the same silver trowel which her late husband had used to lay the foundation stone of S. Luke's thirty-eight years previously. (10) "The day is very fine and many people come," wrote Heath, "collections about £232".

Work began immediately to prepare the ground for the undercroft at the east end. As winter approached building became progressively more difficult. The first snow of the winter fell on November 5th, and the shorter days meant that fires and temporary gas-lights had to be lit to enable work to continue into the evenings.

There were weeks when the site had to be closed down altogether because of severe frost and snow.

By the beginning of February 1886 conditions had improved, the workmen began laying the foundations of the west end of the nave, and the builder's diaries record an average of nine hours a day spent at the Compton site. The undercroft, containing a three-bay arcade running east-west to help support the weight of the chancel floor above, was as yet open to the elements, the brick roof-arches being supported on heavy timber centring frames until they had set properly. During the first two weeks of March there was a series of heavy frosts followed by a rapid thaw. On the evening of Sunday 21st James Heath was getting ready for evening service at Endon church when a messenger arrived from Leek to tell him that one of the arches of the undercroft had given way and fallen in. (11) On arrival at the site he found that nearly all of the arch on the south side had gone, carrying with it the scaffolding and some wrought stone. "God help me," he wrote, "It is dreadful. Never had such a Sunday before." It seems that the brickwork of the arch had been lifted from its wooden supports by the severe frost, and that the sudden thaw had caused it to drop back suddenly, breaking the centring frame underneath. On the next day Heath rose early, walked the four miles from Endon to Leek, and was at Compton by 7 a.m. to begin the work of securing the remaining arches. A week later Norman Shaw visited the church and decided for safety's sake that all the arches should be rebuilt, "as he thinks they will not now set properly after the severe winter".

Like many of Shaw's churches, All Saints' was to have a central tower, low but massive. Interior crossing arches would therefore be necessary, and there was a danger that these might act as a visual impediment between nave and chancel - something the architect wanted to avoid. So the tower was built, not over the choir, but over the last bay of the nave. The western crossing arch is enormously wide (28ft 3 ins), and to keep it visually clear of the lofty chancel arch to the east, it springs from points high above its supporting piers. These piers are free-standing, matching the ones immediately to the west, and they look perilously slender for the tremendous weight thrust on them by the tower. More conventional architects might have inserted transepts at this point, but Shaw continued the aisles for the whole length of the nave and crossing, and to support the tower big flying buttresses were built into the walls and roofs.

It was a clever and daring scheme, and one which Shaw was never to repeat in quite the same way. (12) Its construction presented the builder with his biggest challenge, and he faced it with a characteristic blend of faith and fervour:

Thursday 26th August 1886, "We fix the 2 big springers to the chancel arch today. May God in His infinite mercy grant that the whole may be completed as firmly as the Rock of Ages, Jesus our Saviour."

He also makes mention of the visit of a photographer to the site four days later. A picture taken on this occasion survives, and it shows the work-force standing in front of the partially-built crossing arches: a rare record of a Victorian church under construction.

The tower did, in fact, present difficulties. As the men continued to build over the arches, Heath noticed that the bases of the pillars were cracking under the weight. A few days later two of the temporary wooden frames moved out of position. The fault was not in design or construction, but in the very wet October weather which had softened the ground. A letter from the architect served only to increase Heath's anxiety:

165

Thursday 11th November 1886, " ... I read a letter from R.N. Shaw in which he expresses fear of the tower through this exceedingly wet weather and the tremendous weights being constantly put upon it. God grant that it may stand firmly as a rock. O God help us in our difficulty and danger ..."

No further movements occurred, apart from the minor ones which normally happen as a building settles upon its foundations, but Heath was not the kind of man to take chances. Iron tie-rods ran across the tower arches to help take the strain, and when they were sawn off many years later, one of them cracked like a revolver-shot because of the tension. To help prevent any outward movement in the superstructure of the tower Heath bought an old steel pit rope from a Hanley colliery and laid it between the inner and outer walls, just above the belfry.

Another of Shaw's devices for harmonising nave and chancel was the use of east and west windows of similar proportions. He had tried this for the first time at Meerbrook in the 1870s, but to no great effect. (13) At Ilkley the windows were broadened out to the full width of the nave and chancel, and the same was done at Leek where both east and west windows are of nine lights, filled with tracery worthy of some great cathedral. The delicate patterns in the east window resemble those of a fourteenth-century window in the south transept of S. Oswald's church at Ashbourne, while the west window divides into three groups of three lights each, with lush tracery in the heads.

There is some evidence in Heath's diaries that Shaw's chief assistant, W.R. Lethaby, had a hand in the window designs for All Saints':

Thursday 7th January 1886, "Myself, Son and the Foreman are setting out the Templets for the North and South Chancel windows.

The tracery is very fine indeed. Mr. W.L. Sugden says Mr Lethaby is the finest Architectural Draughtsman in the world."

There are four of these windows, set in pairs, each of three lights, and with delicious curvilinear tracery in the heads. Shaw did in fact leave much of the interior furnishing to Lethaby, who designed the carved frame for the huge reredos. He may also have designed the figures which were to go on it, although the actual painting was done by F. Hamilton Jackson. In any Tractarian church the altar and its furnishings provide the focal point, and a church of the breadth of All Saints' demanded a different kind of altarpiece from the sculpted and carved variety which Shaw had hitherto been content to use. For one thing, there would not be enough vertical space below the east window, so Shaw decided to go for breadth. Bodley and Street had already tried to revive the kind of reredos known as a polyptych - a fixed central panel flanked by pairs of hinged panels opening out to provide a very wide, flat area suitable for figure-painting on a gilded background. Progress had been impeded through lack of suitable painters, but Shaw made a bold decision to install a polyptych at Leek. Hugh Sleigh was willing to pay for it (it cost him £700), and on the day of its arrival in July 1887 James Heath marvelled at its size:

"We go to look at the case containing the reredos for All Saints' Church at Leek Station. It is dreadfully big - 12ft. 6 ins. by 8ft. 6 ins. by 1ft. 4 ins. We can scarcely get it into the church."

When opened out, the frame stretches right across the east wall, a span of just over twenty feet, revealing a complete Calvary scene with soldiers, scribes and Pharisees, mourning women, and the two crucified thieves flanking the central panel showing the dying Christ attended by Our Lady and S. John, with the kneeling figure of S. Mary Magdalene clasping his feet. The quality of the painting was not quite what Shaw had hoped for, but it greatly impressed visitors to the church, and nothing quite like it had been seen in an Anglican church before. (14)

The reredos was fixed on its marble cornice on July 22nd, with just one working day left before the consecration of the church, which the builder describes with surprising brevity:

Monday 25th July, "Day beautifully fine. I go to Compton by 10-37 train and find them almost ready for the Consecration Service. The chancel is beautiful. 2-15 p.m. Consecration Service by the Lord Bishop of Lichfield, and a very imposing one it is, and a grand service by the Bishop. Thank God for permitting me to see and enjoy this day. Amen."

Heath's workmen enjoyed the day too, although in a somewhat different manner, for on July 26th he wrote:

"The masons are not working today because I gave them a half day's holiday to enable them to go to the Service. They have got on the beer and are not now at work; dreadful, isn't it?"

A fair amount of work remained to be done, making pathways around the church, and completing the internal decorations and fittings. Remarkable though All Saints' is for its architecture, its internal décor and furnishings also make it an important landmark in the history of the Arts and Crafts Movement of the late nineteenth century, for two of the leading figures in that movement - William Richard Lethaby and Gerald Horsley - were largely responsible for the interior designs.

The history of the Arts and Crafts Movement is adequately recorded elsewhere. (15) The significant facts here are that the movement was initiated by a small group of architects who in 1884 formed the Art Workers' Guild, and that the five founding members of the Guild were all members or former members of Norman Shaw's staff, including Lethaby and Horsley. They discussed the project with Shaw, and received his encouragement. Concerned at the growing separation of architecture from the other visual arts, and the loss, mainly through the advent of mechanisation, of certain handicraft skills, the Guild aimed at re-integrating architecture, painting and sculpture, and encouraging higher standards of craftsmanship and design. Though inspired by the examples of past ages, the work of many of the Guild's members showed great originality, and a rejection of slavish historicism. This is well-illustrated by the font which Lethaby designed for All Saints' Leek. On entering the church one is faced straight away with an octagonal monolith of polished green marble raised high above the surrounding floor level: a strange intrusion, it may be thought, into a building constructed almost entirely of local stone, yet its simple shape accords well with its immediate surroundings. Around the top there runs a carved frieze made of linked quatrefoils, i.e. a Gothic motif. Just below there is a band of raised lettering in a freely-adapted Lombardic style, while at the base the figures of the four evangelists show a Byzantine influence. By Lethaby too is the pulpit. The underside of the tester has ribs arranged rather like those of a Gothic roof-vault, but in wood. Below, the octagonal pulpit is made of delicately-pierced panels slightly reminiscent of window tracery, separated by richly-carved vertical brackets; all highly original.

The decoration of the chancel is the work of Gerald Horsley. First there is the panelling in the sanctuary, painted in olive-green, with its deeply-carved cornice picked out in gold leaf. After the restoration of Lethaby's reredos in 1954 some well-meaning amateur thought it a good idea to re-touch the gilded parts of the panelling, (16) but he used gold paint, and with catastrophic results that have only recently (1994) been rectified by the expert application of real gold leaf. The chancel would doubtless be much less rich in its decorations had it not been for the generosity of Hugh Sleigh and the executors of Elisabeth Condlyffe (for whom, as we have seen, Shaw carried out work at Meerbrook), who were keen that the work should be completed in the best possible manner. Leek was indeed fortunate in having so many well-to-do families who, in the spirit of the Arts and Crafts Movement, appreciated sound craftsmanship when they saw it, and were prepared to finance it. Horsley's designs for the chancel walls were completed in 1891, and include, on the south side, the Tree of Life flanked by two angels, much in the style of William Morris. The lower walls are decorated with a reticulated pattern incorporating castles, crowns and pomegranates. It bears a striking resemblance to a Pugin wallpaper design of fifty years earlier. Finally, there is the roof, supported on tie-beams, queen-posts and purlins. All of these structural features are decorated, while the ceiling itself is divided into lozenges, one showing the Annunciation, another depicting Christ in glory. These have an icon-like quality, partly because of the gold-leaf background. Other panels have the sacred monogram and worshipping angels, with beautifully-carved and gilded bosses in between. Now fully-restored to its original splendour, the chancel at All Saints' must rank as one of the greatest architectural achievements of the later nineteenth century. Bringing together as it does the architectural genius of Norman Shaw and the artistic abilities of Lethaby and Horsley, it reflects precisely the harmonious partnership between architecture, painting and sculpture which the Art Workers' Guild envisaged. For this reason alone it is the "pioneer church" of the Arts and Crafts Movement. While it draws deeply from the wells of tradition, it is in many ways strikingly innovative. One can look inside Bodley's church at Hoar Cross and enter a fourteenth-century time-warp. One cannot do that at All Saints'.

Gerald Horsley was the designer of the painting on the east wall of the Lady Chapel depicting the Annunciation. The other paintings in the south aisle - on the south wall and over the arches - are the work of J. Edgar Platt, and take us into the twentieth century. The oldest glass in the church is also to be found in the Lady Chapel: the east window done to a Burne Jones design in 1887, and adjacent to it, in the south wall, one by Horsley. In 1893 plans were afoot to fill all the windows with coloured glass. Perhaps one should be grateful that they stopped well short, otherwise the essentially light interior would have been spoiled. The last addition was the great east window which Horsley had always intended to have stained glass to complement the rich colouring of the chancel, but this had to wait until 1923.

The designing of furnishings for All Saints' extended to embroidered altar frontals and vestments. It would have been an easy thing for the church to have done as many others did, and obtain these ready-made from any one of a number of firms catering for the growing demand for such items generated by the spread of ritualism. Not all of such items were in particularly good taste. Instead, All Saints' was fortunate in that the architect and his associates themselves designed many of the soft furnishings, and there was a local organisation - the Leek Embroidery society - more than capable of executing these designs. Here is yet another manifestation of the "Arts and Crafts" spirit; architects, artists and craftspeople assuming collective responsibility, not just for a building, but also for its contents. There was also an unseen hand at work, namely that of William Morris. Not only did his ideals of art and design have a profound influence upon the founding members of the Art Workers' Guild; Morris was also a close friend of the Leek silk manufacturer, Thomas Wardle, whose firm provided the materials for the Embroidery Society. Wardle and Morris spent three years (1875-77) experimenting with dyestuffs for silk, Morris preferring the more natural vegetable dyes to artificial chemical ones. A lost art had to be re-discovered, but eventually at the Hencroft vats in Leek, Wardle and Morris perfected the use of the old organic dyes. Their soft, glowing colours were also fast. Embroideries done by members of the Society with these organically-dyed silks show little sign of fading after a hundred years or more of use.

From about 1868 Thomas Wardle's wife Elizabeth and a group of her friends had been re-discovering another lost art, namely ecclesiastical needlework for which England had been renowned in the Middle Ages. By the 1880s their acquired skills and experience, together with silks spun and dyed in the Wardle factories led to the establishment of the Leek School of Embroidery, and the ability to work to designs submitted to them by artists such as Shaw, Horsley, J.P. Sedding, G.G. Scott, and also William Morris himself. As one might expect, all the Leek churches have examples of "Lady Wardle" embroidery, but the opening of All Saints' provided Elizabeth and her ladies with a unique opportunity. There are six complete altar frontals, two worked to designs by Norman Shaw, a dossal and a funeral pall in red and blue designed by Gerald Horsley, and many smaller items including vestments which, through regular use, have had to be re-worked. It is by any standards an impressive collection, and, thankfully, still being used for the purposes for which it was made over a century ago.

As for the harmonious partnership between architect and builder which contributed so much to the success of All Saints', this came to an end on September 21st 1887 when Norman Shaw visited the church for a final inspection, which was the occasion of a glowing tribute which the builder duly recorded in his diary:

"We have our architect R.N. Shaw here today and we have a good half day at the church, and I am very happy to say he is greatly pleased with the result of our work now it is done. He said to me, 'It is the best and most satisfactory piece of work I have ever had done, and we have to thank you, Mr. Heath, for it; and further, we will yet build a cathedral together.' Thank God for such a kind and encouraging gentleman."

There was to be no cathedral for either of them, although Norman Shaw and G.F. Bodley judged the competition for the Anglican cathedral at Liverpool, and after Bodley's death in 1907 Shaw fought hard to ensure that the contract was given to the young architect they had both chosen - Giles Gilbert Scott.

As for James Heath, 1888 saw a return to the routine of house-building and repair work, having moved his builder's yard to new premises in Shoobridge Street, Leek, not far from the church which is as much his monument as Norman Shaw's. Yet All Saints' was not the last church of its kind to be seen in the Leek area. In 1905 S. Chad's Longsdon was built to the design of Gerald Horsley. It is on a smaller scale than All Saints', but local materials were again used, and the influence of Shaw upon Horsley is unmistakable.

Notes to Chapter 5

1. Andrew Saint, *Richard Norman Shaw*, Yale University Press, 1976, p. 308. This is the authoritative work on Norman Shaw, painstakingly researched and lavishly illustrated.

2. *Leek Times*, 1/8/1885.

3. See *The History of the Leek Embroidery Society*, Dept. of Adult Education, Keele University, 1969, and Anne G. Jacques, *Leek Embroidery*, Staffordshire Libraries, Arts & Archives, 1990.

4. N. Pevsner, "Richard Norman Shaw", *Victorian Architecture*, (ed. P. Ferriday) 1963, p. 245.

5. J. Brandon Jones, "After William Morris", *Artifex*, vol. 4, 1970, p. 53, from which is also taken the quote from Norman Shaw at the start of this chapter.

6. M.H. Miller, *Olde Leeke*, 1891, p. 38 refers to "the palatial residences near to the Cemetery, designed by Norman Shaw, which are also almshouses".

7. The diaries are currently in the possession of the builder's great-grandson, Mr. James A. Smith, of Leek, who has kindly permitted the author to make use of them and to reproduce extracts in this book.

8. Information originally supplied by the late Mr. S.J. Smith, grandson of James Heath.

9. *Leek Times*, 30/7/1887.

10. *Leek Times*, 1/8/1885.

11. *Leek Times*, 27/3/1886.

12. At All Saints' Swanscombe, Kent (1894-5), Shaw built a central tower much in the manner of Leek, but he put stronger piers under the tower arch. At Leek he strengthened the piers with colonettes attached to the sides facing the

aisles, and these are barely visible from the nave, whereas Swanscombe has elongated piers under the tower, visually a less satisfactory arrangement. Shaw used elongated piers at Leek too, but at the west end, where they were not a structural necessity. Together with the narrower arches they mark off the western bay as a narthex/baptistery.

13. The central tower at Meerbrook is over the choir, and there is a strong chancel arch. The chancel is lower and narrower than the nave.

14. Even after re-touching in 1954 the figures still appeared somewhat flat and lacking in contrasts. It was not until he came to build All Saints' Richard's Castle (Shropshire) in 1890 that Shaw found an artist who was able to produce the vigorous kind of painting which the frame and gold leaf background demanded - C.E. Buckridge.

15. e.g. Steven Adams, *The Arts and Crafts Movement*, Tiger Books 1992.

16. Information originally supplied by the late Mr. W. Edge, Verger and Lay Reader at the time this work was carried out.

POSTSCRIPT

No major commemoration or exhibition marked the centenary of Pugin's death. In 1952 the country was preoccupied with other things; mourning the passing of King George VI and preparing for the coronation of the second Elizabeth. When the new Queen opened her first Parliament, few would have recalled that every square inch of the grandeur surrounding her, down to the Throne on which she sat, was the product of one man's creative genius. A year earlier the Festival of Britain had consciously echoed the Great Exhibition of 1851, but there was no place in it for a "Medieval Court" such as Pugin had designed for the Crystal Palace. Britain was in the midst of post-war reconstruction and Gothic architecture - especially Victorian Gothic - was not in vogue. Following wartime damage to the Palace of Westminster, Giles Gilbert Scott's scheme for a fairly conservative reconstruction of the Barry/Pugin buildings encountered violent and bitter opposition, and the "Gothic" party did not have an easy victory. The Blitz had also destroyed one of Pugin's largest churches - S. George's Southwark.

Not all the wartime damage put together can equal the mutilations carried out on some of our finest Gothic Revival buildings in the post-war period by the very people who had the stewardship of them. Changing liturgical fashion, for example, led to the abandonment of the High Altar and the introduction into many churches of a scantily-furnished table of cheap timber, more suited to the pasting of wallpaper than the celebration of the Holy Mysteries. A worse fate awaited the chancel screens which Pugin believed to be so essential a part of the scheme of things but which were never universally loved by his co-religionists. High on the casualty list was the screen at S. Chad's cathedral, and not even the church which Pugin himself paid for and where he lies buried - S. Augustine's, Ramsgate - was immune from the ravages of those who pulled down his rood screen and swept away his altar-fittings.

The Church of England was quick to follow suit. Wrought-iron screens of the highest craftsmanship were removed from Salisbury and Hereford cathedrals, much to the *chagrin* of Sir Nikolaus Pevsner who in 1974 pleaded that Lichfield cathedral be spared a similar act of vandalism, and be allowed to preserve the screen designed by Gilbert Scott in 1859. "Lichfield must hold out until High Victorianism is at last fully appreciated in its best work". And so it has done.

Whether by accident or design, the buildings described in this book have emerged relatively unscathed from the wastelands of the 1960's and 1970's into a more friendly and appreciative environment. S. Giles' Cheadle stands out today not only as Pugin's loveliest church, but as one of the few to have retained all its original furnishings and decorations. The Liturgy for which it was designed - the Latin High Mass - is still celebrated there from time to time, and looking towards the sacristy door on such occasions, one is tempted to imagine that at any moment Pugin himself might emerge - as he was wont to do in several of his churches - clad in cassock and long surplice ready to assist at the altar.

Nationally, Pugin has finally been given the recognition he has long deserved in the form of a major exhibition at the Victoria and Albert Museum during the summer of 1994: *Pugin: A Gothic Passion.* The Exhibition drew together the many strands of his prolifically creative genius: church-building and furnishing, drawing and painting, textile, ceramic and wallpaper designs, jewellery and metalwork, and much more. Equally important was Pugin's influence upon other architects and designers, which is what this book has also tried to reflect locally. Above all, the Pugin Exhibition and the publications which accompanied it attempted to show that the Gothic Revival was not simply - or even primarily - an imitation of past styles, but an ideal encompassing and integrating the whole range of the visual arts, and capable of many interpretations. It may not yet be over. The last thing to be seen in the exhibition was the bold text "Gothic Forever" set over the exit door, as if to challenge a new generation of architects, artists and craftsmen to honour not only Pugin's memory, but also his true principles.

82   The rood screen at S. Giles', Cheadle: **Illustrated London News**, *9th January 1847*